Learning Dapr
Building Distributed Cloud Native Applications

Haishi Bai and Yaron Schneider

Beijing · Boston · Farnham · Sebastopol · Tokyo

Learning Dapr

by Haishi Bai and Yaron Schneider

Published by O'Reilly Media, Inc., 1005 Gravenstein Highway North, Sebastopol, CA 95472.

O'Reilly books may be purchased for educational, business, or sales promotional use. Online editions are also available for most titles (*http://oreilly.com*). For more information, contact our corporate/institutional sales department: 800-998-9938 or *corporate@oreilly.com*.

Acquisitions Editor: Jennifer Pollock	**Indexer:** Sue Klefstad
Developmental Editor: Melissa Potter	**Interior Designer:** David Futato
Production Editor: Beth Kelly	**Cover Designer:** Karen Montgomery
Copyeditor: Rachel Head	**Illustrator:** O'Reilly Media, Inc.
Proofreader: Arthur Johnson	

September 2020:   First Edition

Revision History for the First Edition

2020-08-24:   First Release

See *http://oreilly.com/catalog/errata.csp?isbn=9781492072423* for release details.

978-1-492-07242-3

[LSI]

Table of Contents

Preface

On one gloomy fall afternoon in 2018, Boris Scholl, Yaron Schneider, and I (Haishi) crammed into a tiny phone room at Microsoft's Redmond campus to discuss cloud application development. At the time, we were envisioning a platform-agnostic application model that would allow developers to design the topology of a distributed application in isolation from any specific platforms. The idea eventually became the Open Application Model (*https://oam.dev*), which described an application as a collection of services that were interconnected on a software-defined mesh.

The application model wasn't concerned with how each of the services was written. At that time, I believed coming up with a unified programming model was too ambitious; hence, we tried to strictly define that an application model would always treat a service as a black box. However, as we discussed the idea further, something seemed to be missing.

Suddenly, Yaron jumped to the whiteboard and started doodling. Through his intangible writing, a brilliant idea surfaced, which he called *Reaktive* (*Reactive* with a *k*, reflecting Yaron's deep affection for Kubernetes). The core idea of Reaktive was quite simple—to bring distributed system building blocks to user code through a sidecar container or process. We'll explain how this elegant yet powerful idea brings refreshing thinking into distributed system design and implementation in the Introduction, but for now, back to the story.

A couple of days later Yaron came back with a prototype, and we were blown away. Reaktive brought capabilities such as state management, service discovery, and reliable messaging to user code without polluting that code with any SDKs or libraries; it worked with any programming language (to prove that point, Yaron even did a COBOL sample later on), and it was amazingly lightweight.

For the next couple of weeks the three of us spent a lot of time together brainstorming what functionality it would make sense to add/remove, how we should think about it in the larger Microsoft tech context, and how we would release it. Boris invited architects and developers from within Microsoft and other companies to further validate our thinking and to get early feedback. Overall it felt as if the three of us were on the right path, so we took it to Mark Russinovich, CTO of Azure, and he immediately fell in love with it. He believed the programming model had the potential to have profound impacts on framework design and distributed application development in general—a vision bigger than what we had dreamed of.

Later, Mark proposed that we rename Reaktive to *Actions*, a combination of *Actors* and *Functions*. The name reflected a core value proposition of the new offering: a nonintrusive programming model that unifies stateless service, stateful service, functions, and actors. We all loved the name, so we kept it.

Fast-forward a year, and Actions had gone through months of developments, tons of debates, and numerous early-adopter validations. And eventually, it was ready to be introduced to the world on the Microsoft Ignite keynote stage at Orlando, FL, under a new name: Dapr (*https://dapr.io*), which stands for Distributed Application Runtime. It was one of the most successful open source projects ever initiated by Microsoft. Within the first 24 hours the project collected over 1,000 GitHub stars, and it zoomed by some of the most popular open source projects in just a few days (Figure P-1). The star fever lasted a few weeks before the team members got bored and stopped checking it every few hours.

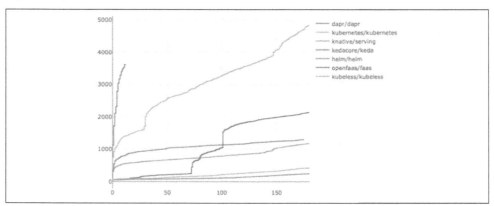

Figure P-1. Dapr's GitHub momentum, tracked with Mark Russinovich's Star Track tool (https://oreil.ly/IG-z9)

Soon we were overwhelmed, as community contributions flooded in from all directions: our partners, competitors, big names, small companies—everybody was chipping in to make Dapr more useful. This was indeed open source at its best.

Coincidentally, Kathleen Carr from O'Reilly contacted me through LinkedIn to see if I had any new book ideas. I proposed an *Actions in Action* book. It was a bold proposal: to write about something that was still being cooked. Kathleen loved the idea, though, and a few weeks later, we'd signed a contract for a book to introduce Actions (now Dapr) to the world.

The fact that you are reading this book proves it was worthwhile to take the risk. Regardless of what would have happened to Dapr, you're here, and we're glad you are.

Resources

- Dapr landing site (*https://dapr.io*)
- Dapr runtime repository (*https://oreil.ly/SRqme*)
- Dapr docs repository (*https://oreil.ly/MlQfS*)
- Dapr samples repository (*https://oreil.ly/7JBHH*)
- Dapr component contribution repository (*https://oreil.ly/lVk5V*)

Conventions Used in This Book

The following typographical conventions are used in this book:

Italic
> Indicates new terms, URLs, email addresses, filenames, and file extensions.

`Constant width`
> Used for program listings, as well as within paragraphs to refer to program elements such as variable or function names, databases, data types, environment variables, statements, and keywords.

`Constant width bold`
> Shows commands or other text that should be typed literally by the user. Also used for emphasis in code snippets.

`Constant width italic`
> Shows text that should be replaced with user-supplied values or by values determined by context.

 This element signifies a tip or suggestion.

 This element signifies a general note.

This element indicates a warning or caution.

O'Reilly Online Learning

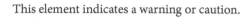 For more than 40 years, *O'Reilly Media* has provided technology and business training, knowledge, and insight to help companies succeed.

Our unique network of experts and innovators share their knowledge and expertise through books, articles, and our online learning platform. O'Reilly's online learning platform gives you on-demand access to live training courses, in-depth learning paths, interactive coding environments, and a vast collection of text and video from O'Reilly and 200+ other publishers. For more information, visit *http://oreilly.com*.

How to Contact Us

Please address comments and questions concerning this book to the publisher:

O'Reilly Media, Inc.
1005 Gravenstein Highway North
Sebastopol, CA 95472
800-998-9938 (in the United States or Canada)
707-829-0515 (international or local)
707-829-0104 (fax)

We have a web page for this book, where we list errata, examples, and any additional information. You can access this page at *https://oreil.ly/Dapr*.

Email *bookquestions@oreilly.com* to comment or ask technical questions about this book.

For news and information about our books and courses, visit *http://oreilly.com*.

Find us on Facebook: *http://facebook.com/oreilly*.

Follow us on Twitter: *http://twitter.com/oreillymedia*.

Watch us on YouTube: *http://youtube.com/oreillymedia*.

Acknowledgments

We'd like to thank all of the Dapr core team who have been relentlessly working on Dapr to make it a production-ready offering: Aman Bhardwaj, Mark Chmarny, Aaron Crawfis, Vinaya Damle, Pruthvidhar Dhodda, Luke Kim, Yotam Lemberger, Leon Mai, Ryan Nowak, Young Bu Park, Mark Russinovich, Shalabh Mohan Shrivastava, Will Smith, Arthur Souza, Charlie Stanley, Mukundan Sundararajan, Ryan Volum, and Ori Zohar. Thank you especially to Mark Fussell and Boris Scholl, who served as technical reviewers for the book.

We'd also like to thank our partners, our early adopters, as well as the fantastic community members who have made great contributions to Dapr.

Introduction

Over the years, many distributed programming models and frameworks have been introduced, such as the Common Object Request Broker Architecture (CORBA), Microsoft Distributed Component Object Model (DCOM), COM+, Java Remote Method Invocation (RMI), Akka, Microsoft Service Fabric actors, and many others. This book introduces our contribution, the Distributed Application Runtime (Dapr), which has been well received by the community so far. Dapr is a new distributed runtime that is under active development. The best way to get up-to-date information is to visit Dapr's official website (*https://dapr.io*). Instead of focusing on API details, this book aims to provide background information on how Dapr is designed and how we see it evolving in the future. We hope the book can help you understand the architecture and design philosophy of Dapr so that you can better apply Dapr in your own applications and make great contributions to the Dapr community.

What Is Dapr?

Dapr is a an event-driven, portable runtime for building microservices for the cloud and the edge. It uses a companion container or process to deliver the building blocks needed by distributed applications, including state management, service discovery, reliable messaging, observability, and more, which will be discussed in detail later. Dapr companion processes, or *sidecars*, expose a standard API surface through HTTP/gRPC protocols. This allows Dapr to support any programming language that supports HTTP or gRPC without requiring any SDKs for libraries to be included in application code. Dapr sidecars are interconnected to form an isolated, distributed runtime for a distributed application, as illustrated in Figure I-1.

When we presented the sidecar architecture to some prospective customers, the idea immediately clicked with several of them. Although our gut feeling told us we were on to something, we spent a fair amount of time discussing why Dapr was necessary, and how Dapr would change the cloud native programming model. The central question was this: Why do we need yet another programming model for distributed applications? Or in other words, what makes Dapr unique and useful? Let's take a look at what it offers.

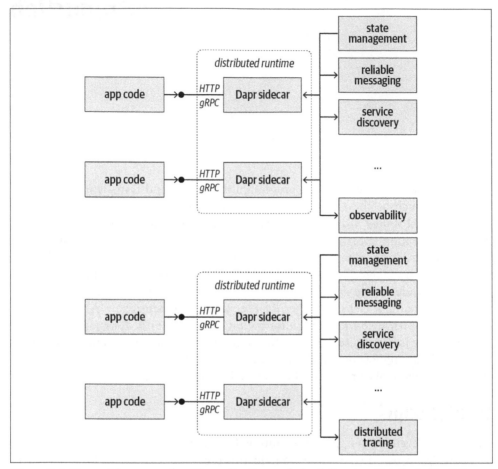

Figure I-1. Dapr sidecars work with application code by delivering distributed building blocks through standard HTTP/gRPC protocols

A Programming Model for a Heterogeneous Environment

A programming model is by definition a set of opinions describing how the designer of the model believes a certain type of programs should be written. The more opinionated a programming model is, the stronger guidance it provides to developers. However, it also imposes a stronger lock-in to a specific framework or implementation, which can be problematic. Modern microservice applications often comprise services written by different teams or external vendors, and there is unprecedented mobility in the modern computing workforce. Getting everyone to buy into a particular programming language or framework is often difficult.

We acknowledge that in the software world of today, we need to embrace variety and seek out ways for developers with different skillsets, working styles, and preferences to work together in harmony. We want developers to be able to express their business logic without fear of vendor lock-in. While seeking a solid common ground for all developer communities, we observed that a microservice, at a high level of abstraction, is a processing unit that exposes some access endpoints, which in turn often talk HTTP. Hence, HTTP seemed like a reasonable common denominator to choose among service developers. For example, to save state with Dapr, all the application code needs to do is send a POST request with a key/value collection as a JSON document to a *state* API provided by the Dapr sidecar. Sending a POST request to a REST API endpoint is such a common practice that we have never encountered any developer who finds it troublesome during our numerous interviews with developers at different skill levels.[1]

Standardizing on HTTP allows maximum interoperability across services written in different programming languages. Throughout this book, you'll see how Dapr enables some unique interoperable scenarios, such as invoking an actor written in a different programming language than the caller.

More Helpful, Less Opinionated

Many existing distributed programming models try to constrain developers to very narrow paths to protect them from making common mistakes in distributed computing. But keeping developers ignorant of the ins and outs of distributed computing is a double-edged sword. On the one hand, it protects them from shooting themselves in the foot. On the other hand, it prevents them from dealing effectively with more complex scenarios. What we often see is that developers try to work around framework limitations, leading to strange and unnatural abuses and antipatterns. Some frameworks even try to create an error-free environment for developers, capturing errors and employing retry or recovery logic to keep the developers oblivious. This means the developers never learn about their mistakes; they keep making the same mistakes repeatedly with the underlying framework silently correcting them, which leads to unnecessary overhead and extra latency.

Dapr tries to be helpful but less opinionated. It delivers common capabilities to developers with default behaviors that are safe for even inexperienced developers to use. On the other hand, it doesn't stop developers from growing their distributed programming skillsets and using advanced constructs as needed. For example, Dapr state management offers optimistic concurrency by default. This allows most transactions

---

1 We introduced gRPC support later. The Dapr API is defined independent from delivery protocols. At the time of writing, we are also considering other wired protocols such as the Data Distribution Service (DDS), especially for IoT scenarios.

to complete without interfering with one another. When conflicts happen, Dapr doesn't try to hide the errors from the developers; instead, developers are expected to handle such errors.[2] Fortunately, handling responses from HTTP requests is also a fundamental skill for web service developers. In the case of a conflict, an explicit 409 Conflict code is returned. The developer can choose to simply forward the response back to client, which is a common practice in web applications (as we don't usually want to do lengthy automatic retries on the server). Thus, exposing the error doesn't necessarily increase the burden on the service developer. On the other hand, if the developer decides to do something with the error, they are welcome to do so. The result is a healthy relationship between the framework and the developer—the developer is left trouble-free most of the time, and they can choose how much they want to be involved in error handling.

Don't Reinvent the Wheel!

Many frameworks try to provide "full-stack" solutions that address every aspect of distributed programming. Because they are fully packaged solutions, they rarely consider how to integrate with others—it's either their way or the highway.

Dapr takes a different approach. Many of Dapr's components are pluggable, including state stores and messaging. This design gives developers great flexibility in choosing what services to use with Dapr. Furthermore, because Dapr allows dynamic binding, developers or operators can choose to bind to different services that are most suitable for the current development context. For example, when an application is deployed on the edge in a disconnected model, it can be bound to a local Redis store running in a Docker container. When the same application is deployed in the cloud, its state store can be bound to a globally replicated data store such as Azure Cosmos DB.

Dapr applies the same principle for reliable messaging. Instead of trying to implement a brand-new messaging system, Dapr is designed to work with proven message buses. Dapr provides a common, HTTP-based facade in front of these message buses, and it pushes configuration management out of the way of developers. This design allows developers to implement reliable messaging with minimal effort, while giving the operations team great flexibility in terms of choosing, configuring, and operating messaging systems.

Dapr uses other open source systems as integral parts, and it works well with popular open source solutions. The Dapr runtime is built on top of proven web frameworks, namely Fast HTTP; Dapr injects itself as sidecar containers while running on Kubernetes; Dapr sidecars work well side by side with service mesh sidecars; Dapr uses

---

2 Dapr does provide configurable automatic retries to handle transient errors. However, it doesn't stop an error bubbling up to app code when the retry policy expires.

OpenTelemetry as the default tracing solution; and the list goes on. Dapr is designed as a hub of building blocks. It was never meant to be a self-contained framework that ships everything from the ground up. This design allows Dapr to surface new capabilities to developers with great agility. It also allows the community to contribute new capabilities to the ecosystem to empower even more service developers.

This open design also makes the Dapr core runtime very lightweight. At the time of writing, it takes about 40 MB of disk space and uses about 4 MB of memory. It runs with 0.1 vCPU cores and adds submillisecond overhead to service invocations. The lightweight runtime reduces resource consumption and improves sidecar injection time. This makes Dapr suitable for dynamically scaled, high-density scenarios such as IoT and big data applications.

Unified Programming Model

There exist different programming models for different types of services: stateless services, stateful services, functions, actors, MapReduce jobs, and others. Dapr doesn't impose hard separations among these service types. Instead, it views all services as processing units that take some inputs and generate some outputs.

> Dapr allows you to write all services in a consistent manner. You can reconfigure services to behave differently later.

Imagine writing a stateless web service, and then reconfiguring it to behave as a function with input/output bindings and hosting it on a serverless environment of your choice. Or, you can make it a stateful service by introducing a state store. And you can further make the service identity-aware, which allows it to act as an actor. Such flexibility has been unimaginable until Dapr.

Many enterprise applications comprise services with different types—say, a stateless web frontend, a stateful backend, and a bunch of workers that are modeled and activated as actors. Developers are often forced to learn all these programming models, or they are tempted to force all service types into the single programming model they are most comfortable with. Although we've seen some successful projects with "pure functions" or "pure actors," most enterprise applications span multiple programming models, frameworks, and even hosting environments.

Dapr offers a unified programming model that delivers capabilities through a standardized HTTP/gRPC protocol. Developers no longer need to target a specific service type when they start to design their service. Instead, when they need certain capabilities, such as state management or bindings, they simply call the corresponding API on the application's sidecar. Even different routes to the same service can assume different roles and present different characteristics. For example, a service can be activated as an instance of an actor, or it can be invoked as a stateful service that provides aggregations across all actor instances.

Another example of the usefulness of the unified programming model is to enable a web service to be triggered by events from popular cloud services through bindings. Figure I-2 demonstrates a photo handler from a web service that is triggered not only by browser clients but also by blob events from both Azure Storage and Amazon S3—without any code changes. The service developer never needs to learn specific service APIs to talk to these services—all the details are abstracted away by bindings.

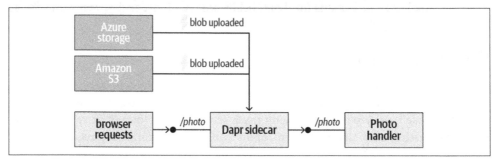

Figure I-2. Dapr bindings

In the remainder of this introduction, we'll give you a brief tour of Dapr's architecture and how it works. The core idea behind Dapr is indeed very simple, but we are pleased to see how a vibrant community is growing rapidly from that simple idea. We hope the idea resonates with you too.

Dapr Architecture

Dapr is made up of the Dapr CLI, a runtime, and a number of control plane services. It also ships with an extensible building block library containing common building blocks such as state stores, messaging backbones, bindings, and observability.[3] We'll cover all these parts in great detail throughout this book, so the following is just a quick introduction to some of them to give you a general idea:

Dapr CLI
> The Dapr CLI is a cross-platform command-line tool that you can use to configure, manage, and monitor your Dapr instances. It also provides access to useful tools such as the Dapr dashboard.

---

3 Dapr is under active development, and the list of components is likely to grow. For example, at the time of writing, we are considering making execution policies and custom middleware pluggable components as well. For an up-to-date component list, please consult Dapr's online documentation (*https://oreil.ly/kY1Vr*).

Dapr host

The Dapr host hosts an instance of the Dapr runtime. The most common form is a Docker container, which is injected into a pod to run side by side with user code on Kubernetes.[4] Dapr can also run in standalone mode as a service process or a daemon.

The Dapr host implements communication protocols such as HTTP and gRPC.

Dapr API

The Dapr API defines the programmable interface to the Dapr runtime.[5]

Dapr runtime

The Dapr runtime implements the Dapr API. It's the core of Dapr's functionality.

Dapr operator

The Dapr operator is a Kubernetes-specific component that supports Dapr's Kubernetes mode. It manages configurations and bindings, which are implemented as Kubernetes custom resources.

Dapr sidecar injector

This component handles Dapr sidecar container injection when Dapr runs in Kubernetes mode.

Dapr placement service

The placement service manages routes to Dapr instances or service partitions. It maintains a route table that directs requests to a specific actor ID or partition ID to the same Dapr runtime instance. See Chapter 5 for details on this service.

Dapr Sentry

Dapr Sentry is a built-in certificate authority (CA) for certificate issuing and management.

Building block: State stores

Dapr saves actor and stateful service state into configurable state stores. Redis is the default local state store, but others, including on-cluster stores, can be plugged into Dapr. There is also a growing list of supported state stores contributed by the community, including Azure Cosmos DB, Cassandra, etcd, Firestore, Memcached, MongoDB, ZooKeeper, and many more. See Chapter 2 for details on how to define and configure custom state stores.

---

4 In this book, we assume you are familiar with general Kubernetes terms and concepts. For a detailed introduction to Kubernetes pods, please see the Kubernetes documentation (*https://oreil.ly/Sgvy7*).

5 Dapr's API surface is growing over time as well.

Building block: Pub/sub

By default, Dapr offers at-least-once message delivery and configures Redis Streams (*https://oreil.ly/7-rl3*) as the messaging backbone for reliable messaging. See Chapter 3 for details on messaging and how you can customize messaging behaviors.

Building block: Bindings

Dapr uses bindings to connect application code to different input and output channels. It defines a very simple binding interface, and it invokes this interface in a single-threaded manner. This design makes writing a new binding a relatively easy task that can often be completed in just a few hours.

Building block: Observability

Dapr is integrated with OpenTelemetry, a set of open source libraries for collecting application metrics and distributed traces. See Chapter 1 for details on how to configure distributed tracing and how to collect application metrics.

You're almost ready to get your hands on Dapr. The getting started samples in the following section use the raw HTTP/gRPC interfaces, but we do also offer a few language-specific experiences, as explained next.

Language Support

Dapr is language agnostic. It offers distributed application building blocks through HTTP or gRPC. However, we do acknowledge the desire many developers have to use language-specific, strongly typed software development kits (SDKs). Out of the box, Dapr ships a few SDKs with actor support in popular languages, including C#, Python, and Java. We expect the community to contribute more SDKs in additional programming languages in the future.

 Even if you choose a language-specific actor framework based on Dapr, your actors will remain interoperable with actors implemented using other Dapr actor frameworks or the pure Dapr runtime.

The Dapr runtime implementation and bindings are developed using Go, the language of choice among the open source community. In theory, additional Dapr API implementations in other programming languages may appear too—we'll leave that decision to the community.

Okay, enough theory already. Now let's put Dapr into action!

Getting Started with Dapr

You have several different options for getting started with Dapr: standalone mode, Kubernetes mode, or one of the language-specific SDKs. The standalone mode is the easiest way to get started on a local machine. The Kubernetes mode is how Dapr will be used in a production environment. Finally, the SDKs get you up to speed quickly with Dapr (especially Dapr actors) in a familiar language. This section walks you through all three paths.

Hello, World! with Dapr Standalone Mode

Observing the prevailing tradition, we'll start our journey with a Hello, World application that listens to a `greeting` event and responds with a "Hello, World!" message.

Getting Dapr on your machine

The Dapr CLI provides an `init` command that can bootstrap the Dapr runtime to your local machine or a Kubernetes cluster. To install Dapr in standalone mode, follow these steps:

1. Make sure Docker is running on the machine. The Dapr CLI uses Docker to run the Redis state store and Dapr placement service.

2. Download the release binary from GitHub (*https://oreil.ly/TeRug*):

   • Windows: *dapr_windows_amd64.zip*

   • Linux: *dapr_liux_amd64.zip*

   • macOS: *dapr_darwin_amd64.zip*

   • Linux ARM devices: *dapr_linux_arm.zip*

3. Extract the Dapr CLI binary to a folder of your choice.

4. Optionally, to make the CLI easily accessible, move the binary to the */user/ local/bin* folder on macOS and Linux, or add the folder from step 3 to your PATH environment variable on Windows.

5. Initialize Dapr by running:

   ```
   dapr init
   ```

The `init` command launches two containers: a Redis container that is used for reliable messaging as well as the default state store, and a Dapr placement service container that manages placement of actors and partitioned services. If you get an error message saying "failed to launch the container," you probably have an existing container that is holding the required ports (6379 for Redis, 50005 for the placement service on macOS/Linux, and 6050 for the placement service on Windows). In such cases, you need to shut down the containers that are holding those ports and try the `init` command again. If everything goes fine, you should see something like:

```
Making the jump to hyperspace...
Downloading binaries and setting up components...
Success! Dapr is up and running
```

Once you've initialized Dapr, you can check the current CLI version and Dapr runtime version by using:

```
dapr --version
```

At the time of writing, that command returns:

```
cli version: 0.1.0
runtime version: 0.1.0
```

Now we can get to our application!

Creating the Hello, World application

It's time to create a Hello, World application. Because Dapr is language agnostic, we'll write sample code in various programming languages throughout this book. You can find code samples in different languages in the Dapr sample repository (*https:// oreil.ly/4_LKA*).

For this example, we'll use Go. Create a new *main.go* file with your favorite code editor (such as Visual Studio Code) with the following contents:

```go
package main

import (
    "encoding/json"
    "fmt"
    "log"
    "net/http"
)

type incomingEvent struct {
    Data interface{} `json:"data"`
}

func main() {

    http.HandleFunc("/greeting",
            func(w http.ResponseWriter, r *http.Request) {
        var event incomingEvent
        decoder := json.NewDecoder(r.Body)
        decoder.Decode(&event)
        fmt.Println(event.Data)
        fmt.Fprintf(w, "Hello, World!")
    })
```

```
        log.Fatal(http.ListenAndServe(":8088", nil))
}
```

This code launches a web server at port 8088, and when it gets a request to the /greet
ing route, it prints out the request body (which it assumes contains a data field) and
returns the string "Hello, World!"

Launching your application through a Dapr sidecar process

In a command line or terminal window, launch a new Dapr runtime instance as the
sidecar process to your application. Note that the dapr run command allows you to
postfix the command line to launch your application—in this case, go run main.go:

```
dapr run --app-id hello-dapr --app-port 8088 --port 8089 go run main.go
```

That command should generate output like the following:

```
Starting Dapr with id hello-dapr. HTTP Port: 8089. gRPC Port: 52016
== DAPR == time="2019-11-11T21:22:15-08:00" level=info msg="starting Dapr Runtime
-- version 0.1.0 -- commit 4358565-dirty"
== DAPR == time="2019-11-11T21:22:15-08:00" level=info msg=
  "log level set to: info"
== DAPR == time="2019-11-11T21:22:15-08:00" level=info msg="standalone mode
configured"
== DAPR == time="2019-11-11T21:22:15-08:00" level=info msg="dapr id: hello-dapr"
== DAPR == time="2019-11-11T21:22:15-08:00" level=info msg="loaded component
messagebus (pubsub.redis)"
== DAPR == time="2019-11-11T21:22:15-08:00" level=info msg=
  "loaded component statestore (state.redis)"
== DAPR == time="2019-11-11T21:22:15-08:00" level=info msg="application protocol:
http. waiting on port 8088"
You're up and running! Both Dapr and your app logs will appear here
...
```

The output shows that the Dapr runtime is launched in standalone mode, it's
connected to an application at port 8088, it's using Redis as the state store and messaging backbone, and it's listening for both HTTP traffic (at the specified port, 8089)
and gRPC requests (at a random port, 52016). Dapr displays its runtime logs and
your application logs in the same terminal window. This allows you to easily trace
interactions between the Dapr sidecar and your application.

Before we continue, let's take a look at the command-line switches we used in the preceding command:

app-id
     Each Dapr sidecar process is identified by a string ID. Dapr runtime instances use
     these IDs to address each other.

app-port
     The application port.

```
port
```
   The HTTP port the Dapr sidecar process listens to.

Table I-1 summarizes the `dapr run` command-line switches available at the time of writing. More detailed information on each of these is provided in Chapter 1, and you can always use the command `dapr run --help` to get the latest information on the supported switches.

Table I-1. dapr run command switches

Switch	Usage	Default
`app-id`	The Dapr sidecar ID	N/A
`app-port`	The application port	N/A
`config`	The Dapr configuration file	N/A
`enable-profiling`	Enables pprof profiling via HTTP endpoint	`false`
`grpc-port`	The Dapr gRPC port	`-1` (random)
`log-level`	Sets the level of log verbosity: `debug`, `info`, `warning`, `error`, `fatal`, or `panic`	`info`
`max-concurrency`	Controls the number of allowed concurrent calls	`-1` (unlimited)
`port`	The Dapr HTTP port	`-1` (random)
`profile-port`	The port for the profile server to listen on	`-1` (random)
`protocol`	Tells Dapr to use HTTP or gRPC to communicate with the app	`http`

Putting Dapr into action

It's time to have some fun with Dapr! The Dapr sidecar provides a `/<version>/invoke/<action-id>/method/<methodname>` route that clients can use to directly invoke a method on your application. For example, a request to the `/v1.0/invoke/hello-dapr/method/greeting` route will be passed to the `/greeting` handler you have in your Go application.

To test this, launch a browser and navigate to this address:

   http://localhost:8089/v1.0/invoke/hello-dapr/method/greeting

You should get back a "Hello, World!" message. Congratulations, you just invoked a web method on your application through Dapr!

Well, maybe that's not very exciting by itself. Later in this book, you'll see how the Dapr sidecar can bring you features like distributed tracing and HTTPS termination without you writing any additional code.

Next, let's make the application stateful. As mentioned earlier, transitioning from stateless to stateful is not always easy with other frameworks, but with Dapr the process is quite natural.

Dapr supports these verbs through direct invocation: GET, POST, DELETE, and PUT.

Adding state

State management is one of the capabilities Dapr sidecars bring to your application. We'll discuss this topic in more detail in Chapter 2, but for now let's go through a quick sample to show you how to turn our Hello, World application into a stateful application. We'll save a simple keyed value into a state store as the application state.

Define the Redis state store. First we need to tell the Dapr sidecar that a state store is available. In standalone mode, you achieve this by adding a state store description file to a *components* folder under the folder where your application is running.

When you run the dapr init command, the Dapr CLI automatically creates the *components* folder with a default Redis state store configuration and a Redis messaging backbone configuration. For example, the following is the default *redis.yaml* configuration file the Dapr CLI generates:

```
apiVersion: dapr.io/v1alpha1
kind: Component
metadata:
  name: statestore
spec:
  type: state.redis
  metadata:
  - name: redisHost
    value: localhost:6379
  - name: redisPassword
    value: ""
```

We'll go over the file schema in Chapter 2. For now, note that the file defines the Redis host address as localhost:6379 without a password. You should update this file to match your Redis settings if you are using a different Redis server.

Update the application to handle state. Your application can request state from the Dapr sidecar through the /*<version>*/state/store name*<key>* route, and it can save state by posting a state object to the sidecar's /*<version>*/state/store name route. When you post state, Dapr allows you to post multiple key/value pairs as a JSON array:

```
[
    {
        "key": "key-1",
        "value": "some simple value"
    },
```

```
    {
        "key": "key-2",
        "value" : {
            "field-a" : "value-a",
            "field-b" : "value-b"
        }
    }
]
```

When you request state back, such as the "key-1" value in this example, you get the value by itself, encoded as a JSON object. In this case, you'd get back some simple value.

Update your application code as shown here:

```
1    package main
2
3    import (
4        "bytes"
5        "encoding/json"
6        "fmt"
7        "io/ioutil"
8        "log"
9        "net/http"
10       "strconv"
11   )
12
13   type stateData struct {
14       Key    string `json:"key"`
15       Value int     `json:"value"`
16   }
17
18   func main() {
19       http.HandleFunc("/greeting",
20           func(w http.ResponseWriter, r *http.Request) {
21           resp,:= http.Get("http://localhost:8089/v1.0/state/statestore/
                 mystate")
22           defer resp.Body.Close()
23           body,:= ioutil.ReadAll(resp.Body)
24           strVal := string(body)
25           count := 0
26           if strVal != "" {
27               count, _ = strconv.Atoi(strVal)
28               count++
29           }
30
31           stateObj:=[]stateData{stateData{Key: "mystate", Value: count}}
32           stateData, _ := json.Marshal(stateObj)
33           resp, = http.Post("http://localhost:8089/v1.0/state/statestore",
34               "application/json", bytes.NewBuffer(stateData))
35           if count == 1 {
36               fmt.Fprintf(w, "I've greeted you " +
```

```
37                      strconv.Itoa(count)+" time.")
38              } else {
39                  fmt.Fprintf(w, "I've greeted you " +
40                      strconv.Itoa(count)+" times.")
41              }
42          })
43          log.Fatal(http.ListenAndServe(":8088", nil))
44      }
```

Now whenever the /greeting handler is called, it requests the state value with a mys
tate key by sending a GET request to http://localhost:8089/v1.0/state/statestore/
mystate (where 8089 is the port on which the Dapr sidecar is listening). Then it increments the value and posts it to http://localhost:8089/v1.0/state/statestore> to be preserved. Next, let's test our application.

Testing the application

To test the application, you need to launch it with the Dapr sidecar:

```
dapr run --app-id hello-dapr --app-port 8088 --port 8089 go run main.go
```

Once the Dapr sidecar is launched, you should see a few new lines in the terminal
window indicating the state store has been found and initialized:

```
== DAPR == time="2019-11-11T22:01:03-08:00" level=info msg="dapr id: hello-dapr"
== DAPR == time="2019-11-11T22:01:03-08:00" level=info msg="loaded component
statestore (state.redis)"
== DAPR == time="2019-11-11T22:01:03-08:00" level=info msg="loaded component
messagebus (pubsub.redis)"
== DAPR == time="2019-11-11T22:01:03-08:00" level=info msg="application protocol:
http. waiting on port 8088"
You're up and running! Both Dapr and your app logs will appear here.

== DAPR == time="2019-11-11T22:01:15-08:00" level=info msg=
  "application discovered on port 8088"
== DAPR == 2019/11/11 22:01:15 redis: connecting to localhost:6379
== DAPR == 2019/11/11 22:01:15 redis: connected to localhost:6379
  (localAddr: [::1]:55231, remAddr: [::1]:6379)
```

Launch a browser and navigate to *http://localhost:8089/v1.0/invoke/hello-dapr/
method/greeting*. As you refresh the page, you should see the greeting count increase.

Now, press Ctrl-C in the terminal to stop both the Dapr sidecar and your application.
This simulates a complete crash of the app (as well as the Dapr sidecar). Then launch
your app with the Dapr sidecar again, and you'll discover that the application state
was preserved. The reason for this should be apparent: the Dapr sidecar saves the
state to the external Redis store.

If you want to check the state saved in Redis, you can use Docker's **exec** command to
connect to the Redis server and query the keys (you can get the Redis container's
name by using docker ps):

```
docker exec -it <name of your Redis container> redis-cli
```

Figure I-3 shows that on my machine, I have a `hello-dapr-mystate` hash key with a data field with the value 6 and a `version` field with the value 7 (we'll explain how versioning works in Chapter 2).

```
C:\Users\hbai>docker exec -it nervous_dirac redis-cli
127.0.0.1:6379> KEYS *
1) "hello-dapr-mystate"
127.0.0.1:6379> HGETALL hello-dapr-mystate
1) "data"
2) "6"
3) "version"
4) "7"
127.0.0.1:6379>
```

Figure I-3. Querying Redis records

Now that you have your application running on a local machine, let's see how to get the same application to run on a Kubernetes cluster.

Hello, World! with Dapr Kubernetes Mode

To demonstrate using Dapr on Kubernetes, we'll create a pair of services: a Python service that periodically sends out messages, and a Node.js service that listens to the messages.

To get stared, you'll need a Kubernetes cluster with role-based access control (RBAC) enabled. You'll also need `kubectl` configured against your cluster.

 This book assumes you are familiar with Kubernetes, so we'll skip any Kubernetes introductions here.

Installing Dapr

If you've got the Dapr CLI installed, you can use the following command to bootstrap Dapr onto the Kubernetes cluster against which your `kubectl` is currently configured:

```
dapr init --kubernetes
```

Or you can deploy Dapr by using Helm:

```
helm repo add dapr https://daprio.azurecr.io/helm/v1/repo
helm repo update
helm install dapr/dapr --name dapr --namespace dapr-system
```

To quickly verify whether Dapr has been configured, use the following command to list the pods in your Kubernetes cluster (you'll need to add the `-n dapr-system` switch to the following command if you used Helm, as the Helm chart deploys Dapr pods under the `dapr-system` namespace):

```
kubectl get pods
```

You should see four Dapr-related pods—`dapr-operator`, `dapr-placement`, `dapr-sentry`, and `dapr-sidecar-injector`—as shown in the following sample output:

```
NAME                                       READY   STATUS    RESTARTS   AGE
dapr-operator-76888fdcb9-x9ljc             1/1     Running   0          10s
dapr-placement-666b996945-dh55v            1/1     Running   0          9s
dapr-sentry-68997bc894-c49ww               1/1     Running   0          10s
dapr-sidecar-injector-744d97578f-dkcbq     1/1     Running   0          9s
```

With Dapr properly initialized on Kubernetes, we can now move on to implementing our message receiver and message sender, starting with the receiver.

Coding the message receiver

We'll write the receiver using Node.js. Instead of initializing the project using npm, we'll create all the application files from scratch. The application is a simple one—it listens to a `/greeting` route and prints out whatever it gets. To get started, follow these steps:

1. Create a new folder named *node_receiver*.

2. Create a new *app.js* file inside the new folder. As mentioned, the application is simple—it listens to POST requests to a `/greeting` route and prints out the request body. As you can see, there's nothing related to Dapr in the following code. This is a simple Node.js server that has absolutely no knowledge of Dapr:

```
const express = require('express');
const bodyParser = require('body-parser');

const app = express();
const port = 8088;
app.use(bodyParser.json());

app.post('/greeting', (req, res) => {
    console.log(req.body);
    res.status(200).send();
});

app.listen(port,
        ()=> console.log(`Receiver is running on port ${port}`));
```

3. Create a new *project.json* file under the same folder, as follows:

```
{
  "name": "node_receiver",
  "version": "1.0.0",
```

```
    "description": "",
    "main": "app.js",
    "author": "",
    "license": "ISC",
    "dependencies": {
      "body-parser": "^1.18.3",
      "express": "^4.16.4"
    }
}
```

Before we go further, let's make sure the Node.js app works by itself:

1. Go to the *node_receiver* folder.

2. Install the required dependencies:

   ```
   npm install
   ```

3. Launch the application:

   ```
   node app.js
   ```

4. Use a tool like Postman to send a POST request to *http://localhost:8088/greeting* with the following JSON payload:

   ```
   {
     "msg": "Hello, World!"
   }
   ```

You should see the message logged on the application's console.

Now it's time to package up the application as a Docker container so that we can deploy it to Kubernetes:

1. Create a *Dockerfile* under the *node_receiver* folder:

   ```
   FROM node:8-alpine
   WORKDIR /usr/src/app
   COPY . .
   RUN npm install
   EXPOSE 8088
   CMD [ "node", "app.js" ]
   ```

2. Build the Docker image using docker build (replace *<username>* with your Docker Hub account name):

   ```
   docker build -t <username>/node_receiver .
   ```

3. Do a trial run by launching the container and then sending a POST request to it:

   ```
   docker run --rm -p 8088:8088 <username>/node_receiver
   ```

4. Once you're done with the test, press Ctrl-C to stop and remove the container.

5. Push the image to Docker Hub (assuming you've logged in to Docker Hub using your Docker Hub account):

```
docker push <username>/node_receiver
```

Now the receiver is ready. Next, we'll move on to the sender.

Coding the message sender

We'll write the sender using Python. It will send a message every five seconds:

1. Create a new folder named *python_sender*.

2. Create a new *app.py* file under the new folder, with the following contents:

```
import time
import requests
import os

n = 0
while True:
    n = (n + 1) % 1000000
    message = {"msg" :"Hello, World! " + str(n)}
    try:
        resp = requests.post("""http://localhost:3500/v1.0/invoke/
            nodereceiver/method/greeting""", json=message)
    except Exception as e:
        print(e)
    time.sleep(5)
```

3. Create a *Dockerfile* under the same folder, with these contents:

```
FROM python:3.7.1-alpine3.8
COPY . /app
WORKDIR /app
RUN pip install requests
ENTRYPOINT ["python"]
CMD ["app.py"]
```

4. Build and push the Docker container:

```
docker build -t <username>/python_sender .
docker push <username>/python_sender
```

This concludes the coding part. Next, we'll create Kubernetes artifacts to deploy both the sender and the receiver.

Creating the Kubernetes artifact

Finally, we are ready to create Kubernetes deployment specifications that deploy both the sender and the receiver container. To do this, follow these steps:

1. Create a new *app.yaml* file with the following contents (be sure to replace *<user name>* with your Docker Hub account name). Note that to enable the Dapr sidecar, you annotate your container deployment with `dapr.io/enabled` and `dapr.io/id`. If you expect to receive incoming calls, you also need to add a `dapr.io/port` annotation. The Dapr sidecar injector reacts to these annotations and injects Dapr sidecar containers into your application pods:

```yaml
apiVersion: apps/v1
kind: Deployment
metadata:
  name: nodereceiver
  labels:
    app: node
spec:
  replicas: 1
  selector:
    matchLabels:
      app: node
  template:
    metadata:
      labels:
        app: node
      annotations:
        dapr.io/enabled: "true"
        dapr.io/id: "nodereceiver"
        dapr.io/port: "8088"
    spec:
      containers:
      - name: node
        image: <username>/node_receiver
        ports:
        - containerPort: 8088
        imagePullPolicy: Always
---
apiVersion: apps/v1
kind: Deployment
metadata:
  name: pythonsender
  labels:
    app: python
spec:
  replicas: 1
  selector:
    matchLabels:
      app: python
  template:
    metadata:
      labels:
        app: python
```

```
      annotations:
        dapr.io/enabled: "true"
        dapr.io/id: "pythonsender"
    spec:
      containers:
      - name: pythonsender
        image: <username>/python_sender
        imagePullPolicy: Always
```

2. Deploy the file using kubectl:

    ```
    kubectl apply -f ./app.yaml
    ```

3. Once the file is deployed, use kubectl to query deployed pods. You should see a nodereceiver pod and a pythonsender pod, as shown in the following sample output. As you can see, each pod contains two containers—one application container and one automatically injected Dapr sidecar container:

    ```
    $ kubectl get pods
    NAME                           READY   STATUS    RESTARTS   AGE
    ...
    nodereceiver-7668f7899f-tvgk9  2/2     Running   0          8m
    pythonsender-5c7c54c446-nkvws  2/2     Running   0          8m
    ```

4. To see if the sender and the receiver are communicating with each other, use the following command (replace <postfix> with the actual pod ID postfix in your environment):

    ```
    kubectl logs nodereceiver-<postfix> node
    ```

    This command generates output like the following:

    ```
    Receiver is running on port 8088
    { msg: 'Hello, World! 2' }
    { msg: 'Hello, World! 3' }
    { msg: 'Hello, World! 4' }
    { msg: 'Hello, World! 5' }
    { msg: 'Hello, World! 6' }
    ```

Now you know how to use Dapr sidecars through the HTTP protocol. In the next section, you'll learn how to use the gRPC protocol instead. If you are not interested in using gRPC, you can skip the next section.

Using gRPC

gRPC is an open source remote procedure call (RPC) system developed by Google. It uses Protocol Buffers (Protobuf), an efficient data serialization mechanism also developed by Google, as both the interface description language (IDL) and the data serialization method. As in other RPC systems, a gRPC client communicates with a gRPC server through a gRPC *stub*, which can be autogenerated using gRPC tools.

A detailed introduction to gRPC is outside the scope of the book. See *https://grpc.io* for more details.

gRPC uses HTTP/2 as the communication protocol. This version has several performance advantages over HTTP/1.1, including features such as proactive data push to avoid multiple requests for resources on a page, multiplexing multiple requests over a single TCP connection, HTTP header data compression, and request pipelines.

Since its introduction, gRPC has gained great popularity in the web services and microservices communities. Dapr is no exception: it uses gRPC for communications among Dapr sidecars and provides native gRPC support for communication with both clients and application code.

It's time for some exercises. In the following walkthrough, you'll use Dapr's gRPC client to invoke a method on a server.

Invoking an Application from a gRPC Client

In this section, we'll create a gRPC client that invokes the /greeting method in our Hello, World service. We'll use the fourth programming language you'll see in this introduction, C#.

Dapr is language-neutral, and to prove the point we'd like to cover as many programming languages as possible in this book. Fortunately, modern programming languages are quite readable in general.

Prerequisites

To complete the following exercise, you'll need:

- .NET Core SDK (*https://oreil.ly/AmV0J*) 2.2 or above
- Visual Studio 2013 or newer, or Visual Studio Code (we've tested the following steps with Visual Studio 2017 and Visual Studio 2019)
- A Git client

Clone the Dapr repository

Since we want to autogenerate a gRPC client, we need to access Dapr's Protobuf definition file (usually with the extension *.proto*). You can get the file by cloning the *dapr/dapr* GitHub repository:

```
git clone https://github.com/dapr/dapr.git
```

As the Dapr repo is Go-based, following Go convention you should clone the repository to your local *$GOPATH/src/github.com/dapr/ dapr* folder.

Create the client application

We'll create a simple C# console application as the gRPC client using Visual Studio:

1. Create a new .NET Core console app named *grpc-client*.

2. Add a few NuGet packages to your project—you'll need these tools to autogenerate the gRPC client:

   - Grpc.Tools

   - Grpc.Protobuf

   - Grpc

3. Add a new folder named *protos* to the project.

4. Right-click on the *protos* folder and select Add°Existing Items. Pick the *$GOPATH/src/github.com/dapr/dapr/pkg/proto/dapr/dapr.proto* file (you can choose to add a link to the file instead of copying the file locally).

5. Right-click on the newly added file and select the Properties menu option. In the Properties window, change the Build Action to "Protobuf compiler" and gRPC Stub Classes to "Client only," as shown in Figure I-4.

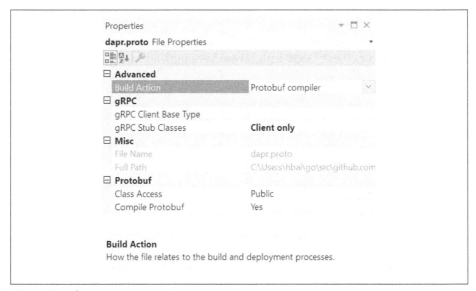

Figure I-4. dapr.proto properties

6. Replace all the code in the *Program.cs* file with the following code:

```
using Google.Protobuf.WellKnownTypes;
using Grpc.Core;
using System;

namespace grpc_client
{
    class Program
    {
        static void Main(string[] args)
        {
            Channel channel = new Channel("localhost:3500",
                ChannelCredentials.Insecure);
            var client = new
                Dapr.Client.Grpc.Dapr.DaprClient(channel);
            Value val = new Value();
            val.StringValue = "Hi, Dapr.";
            Metadata metadata = new Metadata();
            var result = client.InvokeService(new
                Dapr.Client.Grpc.InvokeServiceEnvelope
            {
                Method = "greeting",
                Id = "hello-dapr",
                Data = Any.Pack(val)
            }, metadata);
            Console.WriteLine(result.Data.Value.ToStringUtf8());
        }
    }
}
```

This code uses gRPC to send the string "Hi, Dapr." to a greeting method through a Dapr sidecar at localhost:3500 with ID hello-dapr.

Test the client

For this test, we'll reuse the Go Hello, World application we created earlier:

1. Launch the Go application with a Dapr sidecar. Note that you need to use the grpc-port switch to specify a gRPC port in this case:

```
dapr run --app-id hello-dapr --app-port 8087 --port 8089 --grpc-port 3500
    go run main.go
```

2. In Visual Studio, press Ctrl-F5 to launch the client. The program should stop after printing the "Hello, World!" string.

3. The Go application currently expects a JSON object with a data field. However, the client sends just a simple string. If you'd like the Go application to be able to

---

display the payload correctly, you can update the /greeting handler to directly print the body instead of trying to decode it:

```
txt, _ := ioutil.ReadAll(r.Body)
fmt.Println(string(txt))
```

This concludes the client-side work. We'll move on to the server side next.

Writing a gRPC Server

Now we'll rewrite the Hello, World service to expose a gRPC endpoint instead of an HTTP endpoint. And to keep to the trend of using a different programming language in every example, we'll use Java this time.

Prerequisites

To complete the following exercise, you'll need:

- The Java Development Kit (JDK)
- A Git client
- Maven (*https://oreil.ly/fFCzm*)

Clone the Dapr repository (if necessary)

In this example, we'll use the Protobuf definition in the Dapr repository. If you haven't done so already, clone the repository:

```
git clone https://github.com/dapr/dapr.git
```

Create the server application

The following walk-through uses the Maven command-line tool (mvn). There are plug-ins for IDEs such as Eclipse and IntelliJ, but we feel using the command-line tool offers the most clarity on exactly what's happening. Here are the steps to create the server application:

1. Use mvn to create a new project named grpc-server. Note that the command specifies the group ID as io.dapr, which matches with the Protobuf description file in the Dapr repository—if you want to use a different group ID, you'll need to update your Protobuf description in step 4 to match the parameter value:

    ```
    mvn archetype:generate -DgroupId=io.dapr -DartifactId=grpc-server
    -DarchetypeArtifactId=maven-archetype-quickstart -DinteractiveMode=false
    ```

2. Switch to the *grpc-server* folder:

    ```
    cd grpc-server
    ```

3. Make a new *src/main/proto* folder (for Linux/macOS you need to add the -p switch):

```
mkdir src/main/proto
```

4. Copy *$GOPATH/src/github.com/dapr/dapr/pkg/proto/dapr/dapr.proto* into this folder. We'll reuse this file in this walk-through because it contains the app service definition we need. You can start with your own Protobuf definition files if you prefer, but you'll need to make sure your service definition is compatible with the app service definition in the *dapr.proto* file.

5. Update the *pom.xml* file to include the necessary dependencies:

```
<dependencies>
  ...
  <dependency>
    <groupId>io.grpc</groupId>
    <artifactId>grpc-netty</artifactId>
    <version>1.14.0</version>
  </dependency>
  <dependency>
    <groupId>io.grpc</groupId>
    <artifactId>grpc-protobuf</artifactId>
    <version>1.14.0</version>
  </dependency>
  <dependency>
    <groupId>io.grpc</groupId>
    <artifactId>grpc-stub</artifactId>
    <version>1.14.0</version>
  </dependency>
</dependencies>
```

6. Add the build script to the *pom.xml* file:

```
<build>
  <extensions>
    <extension>
      <groupId>kr.motd.maven</groupId>
      <artifactId>os-maven-plugin</artifactId>
      <version>1.5.0.Final</version>
    </extension>
  </extensions>
  <plugins>
    <plugin>
      <groupId>org.xolstice.maven.plugins</groupId>
      <artifactId>protobuf-maven-plugin</artifactId>
      <version>0.5.1</version>
      <configuration>
        <protocArtifact>
        com.google.protobuf:protoc:3.5.1-1:exe:${os.detected.classifier}
        </protocArtifact>
        <pluginId>grpc-java</pluginId>
```

```
          <pluginArtifact>
          io.grpc:protoc-gen-grpc-java:1.14.0:exe:${os.detected.classifier}
          </pluginArtifact>
        </configuration>
        <executions>
          <execution>
            <goals>
              <goal>compile</goal>
              <goal>compile-custom</goal>
            </goals>
          </execution>
        </executions>
      </plugin>
    </plugins>
  </build>
```

7. Run the Maven build command (mvn). This will generate the source files you need under the *target\generated-sources\protobuf\grpc-java\io\dapr* folder:

```
mvn -DskipTests package
```

8. Add a new *src/main/java/io/dapr/AppServiceImpl.java* file with the following code. This is a typical gRPC server implementation that implements one of the methods defined by the app service (invokeService, which is called when Dapr dispatches a direct invocation request to the app):

```
package io.dapr;

import com.google.protobuf.Any;
import com.google.protobuf.StringValue;

import io.dapr.DaprGrpc.DaprImplBase;
import io.dapr.DaprProtos.*;

public class AppServiceImpl extends DaprImplBase {
  @Override
  public void invokeService(InvokeServiceEnvelope request,
      io.grpc.stub.StreamObserver<InvokeServiceResponseEnvelope>
      responseObserver) {
    System.out.println(request);
    Any response = Any.pack(StringValue.newBuilder()
      .setValue("Hello, World!").build());
    InvokeServiceResponseEnvelope envelope =
      InvokeServiceResponseEnvelope.newBuilder()
      .setData(response).build();
    responseObserver.onNext(envelope);
    responseObserver.onCompleted();
  }
}
```

9. Modify *src/main/java/io/dapr/App.java*:

```
package io.dapr;

import io.grpc.*;

public class App {
  public static void main( String[] args ) throws Exception {
    Server server = ServerBuilder.forPort(8090)
        .addService(new AppServiceImpl())
        .build();

    server.start();
    System.out.println("Server started.");
    server.awaitTermination();
  }
}
```

10. Run the Maven build command again to make sure everything compiles:

```
mvn -DskipTests package
```

Test the gRPC server

The gRPC server is now ready for a test run. In this walk-through, we'll reuse the C# gRPC client we created earlier in this introduction:

1. Build and launch the gRPC server using Maven:

   ```
   mvn -DskipTests package exec:java -Dexec.mainClass=io.dapr.App
   ```

2. Launch a Dapr sidecar. Note that the (application) protocol is set to `grpc` in this case, and that a dummy `echo a` command is used because we are attaching to an existing process:

   ```
   dapr --app-id hello-dapr --app-port 8090 --protocol grpc --grpc-port
     3500 echo a
   ```

3. Run the C# gRPC client from Visual Studio. You should see the request logged by the gRPC server, and the "Hello, World!" message returned to the client.

Before we conclude this introduction, let's briefly examine another Dapr feature—bindings, which are key to enabling the writing of platform-agnostic code.

Bindings

Bindings let you tie your applications to various event sources or destinations. This allows you to write platform-agnostic code that can be dynamically adapted for different environments and contexts. For example, you can use an input binding to bind to an Azure Blob storage container and have the binding triggered whenever a new blob is dropped into the container, or you can use an output binding to invoke an AWS Lambda expression when your service state exceeds a certain threshold. We'll cover bindings in more detail in Chapter 3, but for now, let's do a couple of quick experiments to see how binding works.

Binding in Standalone Mode

One of the key benefits of binding is separation of concerns. When you use bindings, you design your application to receive events from a named event source. However, you don't provide any details about the event source. Then you (or someone who operates your application) can later choose to rebind your application to a completely different event source without affecting your code. As a matter of fact, you can even rebind your applications while they are running.

Dapr ships with a few prebuilt bindings. In standalone mode, each binding is described by a metadata file inside the *components* folder. In the following walk-through, we'll first act as a developer and write a simple HTML page with JavaScript that sends events to a destination named `target`. Then we'll act as an application operator and configure the `target` to be an Azure Event Hub.

Developer: Write a simple HTML page

In this part, we'll write an HTML page with a button. When the button is clicked, the app sends a message to a binding named `target` by making a POST request to the Dapr sidecar with the message addressed to `target`:

1. Create a new folder named *html-app*.

2. Create an *index.html* file under that folder, with the following contents. The code creates a button that, when clicked, sends a POST request to the Dapr sidecar at *http://localhost:3500/v1.0/bindings/target* using jQuery:

```
<!DOCTYPE html>
<html>
    <head>
        <script src="jquery.min.js"></script>
    </head>
    <body>
        <button onclick="postMessage()">Click me!</button>
    </body>
    <script>
        function postMessage() {
            $.ajax(
                {
                    type: "POST",
                    url: "http://localhost:3500/v1.0/bindings/target",
                    contentType:"application/json",
                    data: JSON.stringify({"data": "Hello, World!"})
                });
        }
```

```
      </script>
    </html>
```

Such a POST is possible because the Dapr sidecar allows cross-region requests by default. You can change the behavior by changing the value of the allowed-origins switch (see Table I-1).

Operator: Define an Azure Event Hub binding

Now we'll put on the operator's hat and define what exactly target is. In this walk-through, we'll define target as an Azure Event Hub.

 We assume you are familiar with Azure in general, including how to use Azure Portal and especially Azure Cloud Shell.

Follow these steps to define the Azure Event Hub binding:

1. Log in to Azure Cloud Shell.

2. Create a new Azure Event Hub namespace:

   ```
   az eventhubs namespace create --name <namespace name> --resource-group
      <resource group name> -l <region, such as westus>
   ```

3. Create a new Azure Event Hub event hub:

   ```
   az eventhubs eventhub create --name <event hub name> --resource-group
      <resource group name> --namespace-name <namespace name>
   ```

4. Retrieve the Event Hub connection string. What you will need in step 6 is the primaryConnectionString field in the output:

   ```
   az eventhubs namespace authorization-rule keys list --resource-group
      <resource group name> --namespace-name <namespace name>
         --name RootManageSharedAccessKey
   ```

5. Create a new *components* folder.

6. Add a new *eventhub.yaml* file under the folder. You'll need to replace *<your con nection string>* with the connection string from step 4. Note that you need to append ;*<event hub name>* to the end of the connection string to specify the exact event hub name:

   ```
   apiVersion: dapr.io/v1alpha1
   kind: Component
   metadata:
     name: target
   spec:
   ```

```
type: bindings.azure.eventhubs
metadata:
- name: connectionString
  value: <your connection string>
```

Sending events through Dapr

Now we are ready to send an event to `target` through Dapr. As you can see, the HTML code is oblivious to Azure Event Hub. It simply publishes an event to the Dapr sidecar, which resolves what `target` means and forwards the event to the designated target. To send the event:

1. Launch the HTML page in a browser.

2. Launch the Dapr sidecar:

   ```
   dapr run --port 3500 echo a
   ```

3. Click the Click Me button on the HTML page.

Okay, nothing much happens. However, if you log in to your Azure Portal and observe incoming messages on your event hub, you'll see messages being sent through Dapr, as shown in Figure I-5.

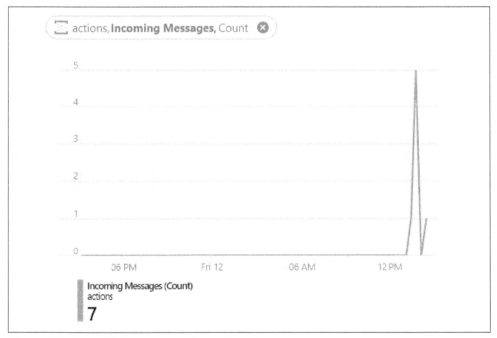

Figure I-5. Event Hub metrics in Azure Portal

Just like any other Dapr feature, bindings work well under Kubernetes. We'll take a quick look at that next.

Binding in Kubernetes Mode

In case you haven't noticed, the *eventhub.yaml* file is a Kubernetes custom resource definition (CRD) file. You can deploy this file directly to a Kubernetes cluster, and Dapr sidecars can pick it up and use it as a binding.

To deploy *eventhub.yaml* to a Kubernetes cluster, use the following command:

```
kubectl apply -f ./eventhub.yaml
```

The Dapr operator service on Kubernetes monitors binding CRDs for changes and notifies all Dapr sidecars in the cluster when a change is detected. This means you can dynamically update your binding definitions to rebind your applications to different sources while the applications are running.[6] This is quite powerful in many scenarios. For example, when you have an edge application that bursts into the cloud, it can be dynamically bound to either edge-based services or cloud-based services to adapt to environment changes.

Summary

This introduction has provided a brief overview of Dapr, a language-neutral programming model that uses a sidecar to deliver microservices building blocks—including bindings, state management, reliable messaging, and actor capabilities—to application code without requiring the application code to include any Dapr-specific libraries or SDKs.

A key goal of Dapr is to abstract infrastructural details away from developers. Through Dapr building blocks, application code is completely isolated from the underlying infrastructure, allowing the application to be configured and reconfigured on different platforms at operation time without needing to change the application code. This is a powerful feature that enables scenarios such as edge and multicloud applications.

We hope you find Dapr interesting. Throughout the rest of the book, we'll expand on all the Dapr components and cover various application scenarios with Dapr. We'll also introduce how to extend Dapr in various ways. We hope you join the community to help make Dapr a simple, efficient, and powerful distributed programming model for everyone!

---

6 At the time of this writing, the Dapr team is still deciding on the exact behavior of picking up new CRD changes—whether this needs a container restart. Please see the online documentation for latest updates.

CHAPTER 1

Services

The basic computing unit in a Dapr-enabled application is a service. One of the goals of Dapr is to enable you to write these services in the way you like with the language of your choice. Dapr sits side by side with your services and brings in necessary capabilities such as state management, tracing, and secured communication when you need them. This chapter walks you through how various Dapr features came to be.

The World Before Cloud

Around the year 2000, I (Haishi) was working at a financial software company in San Francisco. On the second floor there was a server room, which required a special key card to access. The room was always freezing cold and noisy. It hosted everything the company needed to operate—domain controller, mail servers, file servers, source repositories, databases, test labs, and all the HR records. Other than the server racks, the room was filled with shelves of tapes stacked up to the ceiling. The company backed up the servers regularly, and all the backups were stored on these tapes. The room was also equipped with huge tanks of pure nitrogen gas, which would be released to save the room in case of fire.

The IT staff were very protective of the servers. And they were frequently annoyed by developers' requests to deploy new service versions—after all, keeping the CEO's mailbox working was a higher priority. Deploying a new version was a major operation: servers were backed up, databases were backed up, servers were patched, data migration scripts were executed, validation tests were executed. And if the tests failed, everything got rolled back, and the IT guys gave us the evil eye. Their pagers beeped, and they told us they could only do another deployment tomorrow.

At the time, the browser/server (B/S) architecture was on the rise and set to replace the established client/server (C/S) architecture. The main promise of the B/S architecture was to enable smooth client adoption by making the clients as thin as a web browser. As more and more companies tried to adopt a subscription-based business model instead of the traditional license-based business model, B/S architecture concentrated large amounts of compute resources back into centralized servers. These servers were critical to business. However, managing them became an increasingly hard problem. The companies had to go through extensive capability planning processes to ensure that they could purchase enough servers that would satisfy their requirements without blowing the budget. At the same time, because the services had to be kept available during updates and server failures, the companies needed the ability to quickly and consistently deploy and update their applications with minimal interruptions to running services.

Cloud Promises and Challenges

A few years later, the cloud rose to the challenge of running highly available hosted services. It promised availability and elasticity, offering consumption-based pricing and infinite capacity. However, these promises didn't come for free. They imposed some new requirements on how applications were designed.

Availability

Cloud computing achieves high availability through redundancy. Cloud servers are not magical—they fail just like the servers in your own datacenters. But when a cloud server fails, the provider won't have enough human resources to diagnose and fix the server problem on the fly. Instead, they'll simply pull another server from their enormous server pool and migrate your application over, and it will continue as usual.

This means that at any time, your application might be stopped and restarted on a brand-new server instance. This raises some challenges in terms of how you design your services. For example, if you accumulate in-memory state, the state will be lost when the restart happens. If your service takes a long time to be initialized, service availability will be affected as well. Furthermore, if you save some state locally, such as by writing a file to a local drive, that state will be lost when the migration happens. Migrating state is always troublesome. Therefore, many cloud workload management systems require the applications to be *stateless*, which means these applications don't save any local state to the hosting environment.

Moving application bits from one server to another takes time. If an application can be broken down into smaller pieces, moving and restoring those smaller pieces is much more efficient. Using these smaller services, sometimes referred to as *microservices*, is becoming the de facto way of composing applications. Microservices are usually loosely coupled, because they should remain functional as their peers are being moved and restarted.

If your service must be *stateful*, which means it must save some local state, the state needs to be replicated to ensure availability. In such cases, a single writer instead of multiple writers is often used to avoid data conflicts.

Elasticity

When the demands of a service exceed the capacity of the hosting server, there are two possible solutions: the service can be migrated to a more powerful server, or multiple copies of the service can be deployed to share the workload. The latter approach, which is called *scaling out*, is the preferred way to scale in the cloud. Because cloud providers have huge numbers of servers, a service in theory can be scaled out infinitely. On the flip side, when the workload diminishes, a service can be *scaled in* to release unused compute capacity. Because you pay for what you consume in the cloud, such elasticity can be a major cost saver if you have seasonal heavy loads (such as in retail businesses) or occasional spikes (such as in news businesses) in your workloads.

For simple web APIs, scaling out is relatively straightforward. This is because each web request is often self-contained, and data operations are naturally segmented by transaction scopes. For such APIs, scaling out can be as simple as adding more service instances behind a load balancer. However, not all applications are designed to be scaled out. Especially when a service assumes it has full control of the system state, multiple instances of the service may make conflicting decisions. Reconciling such conflicts is a hard problem, especially when prolonged network partitioning happens. The system is then said to have a "split brain," which often leads to irreconcilable conflicts and data corruption.

Partitioning is an effective way to scale out a service. A large workload can often be split into multiple partitions along logical or physical boundaries, such as by customers (or tenants), business units, geographic locations, countries, or regions. Each of the partitions is a smaller system that can be scaled in or out as needed. Partitioning is especially useful when scaling a stateful service. As mentioned before, the state of a stateful service needs to be replicated to ensure availability. Partitioning controls the amount of data being replicated and allows parallel replication because all replication operations are scoped to partitions.

Partitions can be either *static* or *dynamic*. Static partitioning is easier in terms of routing, as routing rules can be predetermined. However, static partitioning may lead to unbalanced partitions, which in turn lead to problems such as overstressed hotspots and underutilized server capacity. Dynamic partitioning dynamically adjusts partitions using techniques such as consistent hashing (*https://oreil.ly/VFvWj*). Dynamic partitioning usually can ensure evenly distributed workloads across partitions.

However, some partition-aware routing logic is needed to route user traffic to the appropriate partitions. It's also hard to ensure data separation, which is required by some compliance standards, on dynamic partitions. When you design your services, you need to decide on a partitioning strategy based on both your technical and non-technical needs and stick to it, because changing partitioning strategies later is often difficult, especially when you have constant incoming data streams.

Cloud Native Applications

Cloud native applications are designed to be operated in a cloud environment. For an application to be considered "cloud native," it should present the following characteristics:

Automatically deployable

A cloud native application can be consistently redeployed when necessary. This feature is required when automatic failover is enabled to ensure high availability. Virtualization and containerization allow applications to be packaged as self-contained packages that can be deployed on different hosting nodes without possible conflicts in external dependencies. These packages must be deployable without human intervention because the failover mechanism may get triggered at any time due to different conditions such as machine failures and compute resource rebalancing.

As mentioned previously, moving a stateless service to a new machine is simpler than moving a stateful service, and being able to launch a new service instance quickly is key to improving availability. However, being stateless is not a mandatory requirement of a cloud native application. Techniques such as partitioning enable stateful service instances to be moved efficiently as well.

Isolation among components

A component in a multicomponent cloud native application should continue to operate when other components fail. Although the component may be unable to deliver the required functionality, it should be able to restore to a fully functional state when all dependent services come back online. In other words, a failing component or a restarting component should not cause cascading errors in other components.

Such isolation is usually achieved by a combination of clearly defined APIs, client libraries with automatic retires, and loosely coupled design through messaging.

Isolation among components also means the components should be individually scalable. The consumption-based model requires cloud native application operators to fine-tune the resource consumptions of individual components to better meet the requirements with minimum resource consumption. This requires components to be adaptive to workload changes when related components are being scaled.

Cloud native applications are usually composed of microservices (in fact, the two terms are often thought of as synonymous). Despite the name, microservices don't have to be small—the concept is all about operations. Microservices applications are isolated, consistently deployable, and easy to scale, making them ideally suited to a cloud environment.

Infrastructure Is Boring

For a cloud platform to fulfill the promise of availability and elasticity, workloads must be separated from the underlying infrastructure so that infrastructure can be mobilized as needed for common cloud operations such as failover and scaling. Infrastructural concerns should be the last thing on a developer's mind. Projects such as Open Application Model (OAM, discussed later in this chapter) and Dapr aim at providing developers tools and abstractions so that they can design and develop applications that are agnostic to the underlying infrastructure, for both cloud and edge deployment.

Dapr and containers

Containerization provides a lightweight isolation mechanism for workloads, and Kubernetes offers powerful workload orchestration on clustered compute nodes. Dapr is designed to work natively with containers and Kubernetes. However, as you saw in the previous chapter, Dapr works in noncontainerized environments as well. The primary reason for this design is to support IoT scenarios and legacy scenarios in which containers are not used. For example, a legacy system running on a virtual machine or a physical server can use a Dapr process, which can be configured as a Windows service or a Linux daemon. You can run the Dapr runtime as an independent container as well, and because it's lightweight it can easily be deployed to devices with lower capacities.

Regardless of how you deploy your Dapr sidecars, the sidecars provide local service endpoints that bring various capabilities to your application that you can leverage without needing to worry about any infrastructural details—this is the key value of Dapr. A cloud native application often uses various cloud-based services, such as storage services, secret stores, authentication servers, messaging backbones, and more. Dapr abstracts these services into simple interfaces so that your applications can be reconfigured to use different service implementations, including containerized services and hosted services, in different deployment environments.

IaaS, PaaS, SaaS, and serverless

Many cloud projects start with a debate over which tier of the cloud—IaaS, PaaS, or SaaS—should be the entry point. We'll take SaaS (Software as a Service) out of the discussion for now, because from an application's perspective, using SaaS means calling a hosted API. This doesn't affect how the application itself is hosted.

IaaS (Infrastructure as a Service) gives you the most flexible control over the compute resources you provision in the cloud. Because you're working at the infrastructural level, you can tailor your hosting environment in the exact way you want. You can choose the network topology, operating system, runtime, frameworks, and more. Then you deploy your application on the specified infrastructure and manage it just as you would in a local datacenter. Working at infrastructural level, however, makes it harder to take advantage of the cloud's availability and elasticity features. For example, although your cloud provider can automatically restore a failed virtual machine and trigger a redeployment of your application, the time it takes to build up the environment could be lengthy, causing unexpected outages.

PaaS (Platform as a Service) is more opinionated. When you follow the programming models chosen by a PaaS platform, many infrastructural burdens are taken off your shoulders. Dapr is designed to work with different PaaS platforms. Architecturally, Dapr is just a set of service endpoints your application can use. In a way, it's a "local SaaS" that your application can consume. It doesn't mandate how your application is written, or which frameworks your application uses.

Because Dapr runs as a sidecar, it will work with any serverless platform that supports the concept of grouped containers. This includes different flavors of managed Kubernetes clusters as well as Azure Container Instances (ACI), which supports container groups. To run on a serverless platform that doesn't support container groups, you can package the Dapr process as part of your application container.

With these discussions in mind, we'll now introduce how Dapr provides service invocation abstractions among distributed components. The service invocation feature provides the fundamental supports that allow components in a microservices application to communicate with each other.

Service Invocation

Multiple services can communicate with each other through Dapr sidecars, as shown in Figure 1-1. When service *a*, represented by a Dapr sidecar named *dapr-a*, tries to call a method foo defined by service *b*, represented by a Dapr sidecar named *dapr-b*, the request goes through the following steps:

1. Service *a* sends a request to its own Dapr sidecar through *localhost:3500* (assuming the sidecar listens to port 3500) with path */v1.0/invoke/<target Dapr ID>/ method/<target method>*. Note that a service always sends the invocation request to its own Dapr sidecar through *localhost*.

2. The *dapr-a* sidecar resolves the address of the *dapr-b* sidecar and forwards the request to *dapr-b*'s invocation endpoint.

3. The *dapr-b* sidecar invokes service *b*'s /foo route.

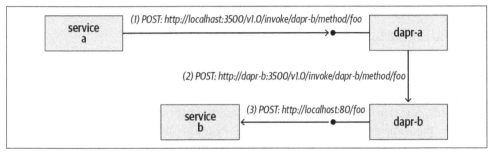

Figure 1-1. Service invocation through Dapr sidecars

Name Resolution

The first step required to invoke another service is to locate the service. Each Dapr sidecar is identified by a string ID. The task of name resolution is to map the Dapr ID to a routable address. By default, Dapr uses the Kubernetes name resolution mechanism when running on Kubernetes, and it uses multicast DNS (mDNS) while running in local mode. Dapr also allows other name resolvers to be plugged into the runtime as a component.

Kubernetes

When you deploy a pod with Dapr annotations, Dapr automatically injects a Dapr sidecar container into your pod. It also creates a ClusterIP service with a -dapr postfix. To verify this, use kubectl to deploy the following pod spec from Dapr's sample repository (*https://oreil.ly/Z7l6H*):

```
apiVersion: apps/v1
kind: Deployment
metadata:
  name: pythonapp
  labels:
    app: python
spec:
  replicas: 1
  selector:
    matchLabels:
```

```
      app: python
  template:
    metadata:
      labels:
        app: python
      annotations:
        dapr.io/enabled: "true"
        dapr.io/id: "pythonapp"
    spec:
      containers:
      - name: python
        image: dapriosamples/hello-k8s-python
```

Then you can use kubectl to view the created service:

```
kubectl get svc pythonapp-dapr
NAME              TYPE        CLUSTER-IP    EXTERNAL-IP   PORT(S)           AGE
pythonapp-dapr    ClusterIP   10.0.79.144   <none>        80/TCP,50001/TCP  11m
```

By default, Kubernetes uses CoreDNS for name resolution. The following commands create a busybox pod in your cluster and examine the default name resolution configuration:

```
kubectl apply -f https://k8s.io/examples/admin/dns/busybox.yaml
kubectl exec busybox cat /etc/resolv.conf
```

In our environment, which is hosted on Azure Kubernetes Service (AKS), they produce the following output:

```
nameserver 10.0.0.10
search default.svc.cluster.local svc.cluster.local
  cluster.local vvdjj2huljtelaqnqfod0pbtwh.xx.internal.cloudapp.net
options ndots:5
```

You can manually look up the service address using the following command:

```
kubectl exec -ti busybox -- nslookup pythonapp-dapr
```

This command generates the following output in our environment. You should get similar results in yours, except for the resolved service IP. The output shows how Dapr can resolve the Dapr ID, pythonapp-dapr, to the corresponding service to be invoked:

```
Server:    10.0.0.10
Address 1: 10.0.0.10 kube-dns.kube-system.svc.cluster.local

Name:      pythonapp-dapr
Address 1: 10.0.79.144 pythonapp-dapr.default.svc.cluster.local
```

When the pod is scaled out, traffic to the service is evenly distributed among the instances—this is how a Dapr sidecar scales out.

mDNS

The multicast DNS protocol is used to resolve hostnames to IP addresses on a small network by broadcasting UDP packets. Essentially, each participant announces its own address and updates its DNS lookup cache based on what its peers announce. When running in local mode, Dapr uses mDNS for name resolution.

When multiple Dapr sidecars run on the same host, they need to listen to different HTTP/gRPC ports to avoid port conflicts. In such cases, mDNS resolves to the specific port the Dapr instance is listening to. For example, the Dapr ID dapr-a may get resolved to *localhost:3500*, and the Dapr ID dapr-d may get resolved to *localhost:3600*.

At the time of writing, Dapr's mDNS implementation (*https://oreil.ly/Ww3hh*) is constrained to a single host. Chances are, by the time you're reading this text, the implementation will have been extended to support multiple machines on the same local network. Until that happens, Dapr's local mode supports only Dapr sidecars running on the same host, listening to different ports. After the extension, Dapr sidecars running on the same local network will be able to address each other through Dapr IDs.

Requests and Responses

Dapr forwards all request headers as well as query parameters for HTTP requests, and all metadata associated with gRPC requests. Although services can talk to Dapr through either HTTP or gRPC, Dapr sidecars always communicate with each other through gRPC. When converting an HTTP request to a gRPC request, all HTTP headers are encoded into the headers metadata element of the gRPC request. Dapr supports common HTTP verbs including GET, POST, DELETE, and PUT.

Dapr uses mutual TLS to secure communications among sidecars. Dapr sidecars authenticate with each other with sidecar-specific certificates that are rooted to a cluster-level CA (when running on Kubernetes), or a customer-supplied root certificate—see Chapter 4 for details. The communication between a service and its associated sidecar is often unprotected as the sidecar is assumed to be in the same security domain as the service, but you can configure end-to-end encryption between two services through Dapr.

Concurrency Control

The Dapr runtime supports a max-concurrency switch. When set to a positive value, this controls how many concurrent requests can be dispatched to a user service. Once the number of concurrent requests exceeds the given threshold, additional requests will be held in flight until additional processing capacity is freed up. This means a client request may time out due to a busy service.

Service Invocation Experiment

In this section, we'll conduct a small service invocation experiment. We'll use PHP here, but remember that you can pick any language you like; all you need to do is to write a simple web server without any Dapr-specific logic or libraries.

Creating the PHP service

The first step is to create a simple PHP web service. This service responds to any requested routes and returns the request method, request path, and request headers:

1. Create a new folder named *php-app*.

2. Under the *php-app* folder, create a new PHP script file named *app.php* with the following contents:

   ```php
   <?php

   $method = $_SERVER['REQUEST_METHOD'];
   $uri = $_SERVER['REQUEST_URI'];

   $headers = array();
   foreach ($_SERVER as $key => $value) {
       if (strpos($key, 'HTTP_') == 0 && strlen($key) >5) {
           $header = str_replace(' ', '-', ucwords(str_replace('_', ' ',
             strtolower(substr($key, 5)))));
           $headers[$header] = $value;
       }
   }

   echo json_encode(array('method'=>$method, 'uri' => $uri,
     'headers' => $headers));

   ?>
   ```

3. Under the same folder, create a *Dockerfile* with these contents:

   ```
   FROM php:7.4-cli
   COPY . /usr/src/myapp
   WORKDIR /usr/src/myapp
   CMD ["php", "-S", "0.0.0.0:8000", "app.php"]
   ```

4. Build and push the Docker image:

   ```
   docker build -t <image tag> .
   docker push <image tag>
   ```

Deploying the service

The next step is to create a Kubernetes deployment spec to deploy the PHP service. You'll also define a LoadBalancer service so that you can access the service through a public IP:

1. Create a new *php-app.yaml* file with the following contents:

```
kind: Service
apiVersion: v1
metadata:
  name: phpapp
  labels:
    app: php
spec:
  selector:
    app: php
  ports:
  - protocol: TCP
    port: 80
    targetPort: 8000
  type: LoadBalancer
---
apiVersion: apps/v1
kind: Deployment
metadata:
  name: phpapp
  labels:
    app: php
spec:
  replicas: 1
  selector:
    matchLabels:
      app: php
  template:
    metadata:
      labels:
        app: php
      annotations:
        dapr.io/enabled: "true"
        dapr.io/id: "phpapp"
        dapr.io/port: "8000"
    spec:
      containers:
      - name: php
        image: <image tag>
        ports:
        - containerPort: 8000
        imagePullPolicy: Always
```

2. Deploy the file using `kubectl`. Then get the public IP of the `phpapp` service:

```
kubectl apply -f php-app.yaml
kubectl get svc phpapp
```

3. Use a browser or Postman to send a request to *http://<your service ip>/abc/def?param=123*. You should get a JSON document that is similar to the following:

```
{
  "method":"GET",
  "uri":"\/abc\/def?param=123",
  "headers":{
        ...
  }
}
```

Exposing the -dapr service

As mentioned previously, when you deploy a pod with Dapr annotations Dapr creates a `-dapr` `ClusterIP` service. For this experiment, you'll edit the service to change its type to `LoadBalancer`, which means it will be assigned a public IP through the load balancer:

```
kubectl edit svc phpapp-dapr
```

Replace `ClusterIP` in this file with `LoadBalancer` and then save the file. `kubectl` should report that the service has been edited:

```
service/phpapp-dapr edited
```

Wait for a public IP to be assigned to `phpapp-dapr`. Then you can invoke the PHP service through the exposed Dapr service:

http://<dapr service IP>/v1.0/invoke/phpapp/method/foo

You can experiment with combinations of different request paths, parameters, and request headers. You'll be able to observe how Dapr forwards the metadata to the PHP service.

The Universal Namespace

At the time of writing, we are designing a new Dapr capability tentatively called the *universal namespace*. So far, Dapr name resolution and communication work only in a single cluster. However, we'd like to extend Dapr so that it supports name resolution and communication across multiple clusters.

The idea of the universal namespace is to allow users to postfix service names with cluster identifiers so that services on different clusters can address each other through names such as `<service name>.<cluster identifier>`. For example, to invoke a method `foo` on `service-1` on `cluster1`, a client would simply send a POST request to a Dapr endpoint at *http://localhost:3500/v1.0/invoke/service-1.cluster1/foo*.

Because Dapr sidecars are often exposed as `ClusterIP` services, we plan to introduce a new Dapr gateway service that can be associated with a public IP. Name resolution through DNS will resolve to the gateway service address, and the gateway will forward the request to local services. Of course, if you choose to expose a Dapr service with a public IP, the DNS records on the other cluster can be updated to directly route the traffic to the target service without going through the gateway.

To secure communication across clusters, root certificates of the clusters (or a shared root certificate) are exchanged for mutual TLS authentication.

 We'll talk more about this and other up-and-coming Dapr features in Chapter 7.

Pub/Sub

Microservices architectures advocate for loosely coupled services. When a service invokes another service through Dapr, it doesn't need to resolve the physical service address itself. Instead, it can simply refer to another service through the corresponding Dapr ID. This design allows great flexibility in service placement. However, the calling service still needs to know the exact name of the target service.

Many modern applications comprise multiple services that are developed and operated by different teams. Especially in large enterprise environments, different services may have different life cycles, and a service may get replaced by a completely different service. Maintaining direct connections among these services can be difficult, if not impossible. We therefore need ways to keep services loosely coupled but efficiently integrated as a complete application.

To achieve better loose coupling, Dapr supports *message-based integration patterns*. Before we dive into how Dapr provides messaging support, let's recap the benefits of this approach.

Benefits of Message-Based Integration

Message-based integration allows services to exchange messages through a messaging backbone, as shown in Figure 1-2. Instead of sending requests directly to one another, all services communicate with each other by exchanging messages through the messaging backbone. This additional level of indirection brings many desirable characteristics, as summarized in the following subsections.

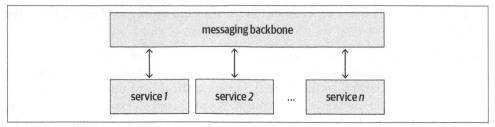

Figure 1-2. Message-based integration

Alleviating performance differences

Different services have different throughputs. If all services are chained together through direct invocations, the overall throughput of the system is determined by the slowest service in the chain. This is usually unacceptable. For example, a web service should remain responsive to take new orders as the backend service processes orders, which may take much longer.

In such cases, the frontend service can take a new order, put it to a processing queue, and get ready to take the next order. At the same time, the backend service can pick up and process orders at its own pace, without affecting the responsiveness of the frontend service. Furthermore, the backend service can be independently scaled out to drain the processing queue faster.

Advanced queuing features such as deduplication (removing duplicate requests), priority queuing (bumping higher-priority requests to the front of the queue), and batching (combining requests together into a single transaction) can help to further optimize the system.

Improving availability

Message-based integration can also help improve system availability in some cases. For instance, when the backend is brought down for maintenance or upgrade, the frontend can keep taking new requests and queue them.

With a globally redundant messaging backbone your system can even survive regional failures, because the queued requests remain available even when all your system components fail. They can be picked up when the system restarts.

Some queuing systems allow checking out a work item without removing it from the queue. Once the work item is checked out, the processor is given a time window to process it and then remove it from the queue. If the processor fails to do so in the allotted time, the work item will be made available for others to check out. This is an implementation of *at-least-once* message delivery and ensures a work item is processed at least once.

Flexible integration topology

You can implement various service topologies through message-based integration: pub/sub, bursting to cloud, content-based routing, scatter-gather, competing consumer, dead letter channel, message broker, and many more.

In the pub/sub pattern, publishers publish messages to a topic to which subscribers subscribe. Figure 1-3 illustrates some of the integration topologies you can achieve with pub/sub.

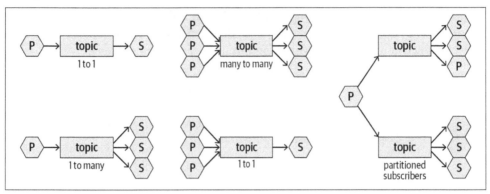

Figure 1-3. Integration patterns with pub/sub

One of the major benefits of pub/sub is that the publishers and subscribers are totally decoupled (well, to be exact, they are still coupled by message format, but we're just talking about topology here). A publisher never cares how many subscribers subscribe to the topic it publishes to, or who the subscribers are. The same applies to the subscribers. This means publishers and subscribers can be evolved or replaced at any time without affecting each other. This is quite powerful, especially when multiple teams are trying to work together to deliver a complex application.

Pub/Sub with Dapr

To subscribe to topics, your application should send a GET request to the Dapr side-car with a list of topics and corresponding routes as a JSON array, as shown in the following Node.js sample code:

```
app.get('/dapr/subscribe', (_req, res) => {
    res.json([
      {
        topic: "A",
        route: "A"
      },
      {
        topic: "B",
        route: "B"
      }
```

```
    ]);
});
```

Then the sidecar sends you events through POST requests when publishers publish content to the subscribed-to topics:

```
app.post('/A', (req, res) => {
    console.log("A: ", req.body);
    res.sendStatus(200);
});
```

To publish to a topic, your application should send a POST request to a /publish/ <topic> endpoint on your Dapr sidecar with the message to be sent as the POST body, wrapped as a CloudEvent (more on this in the following section):

```
const publishUrl = `http://localhost:3500/v1.0/publish/<topic>`;
request( { uri: publishUrl, method: 'POST', json: <message> } );
```

> You can get the source code of a complete pub/sub sample from Dapr's sample repository (*https://oreil.ly/rB7xE*).

How Pub/Sub Works

Pub/sub needs a messaging backbone. However, as explained in the Introduction, one of Dapr's design principles is to not reinvent the wheel. So instead of creating a new messaging backbone, Dapr is designed to be integrable with many popular messaging backbones, including Redis Streams, NATS, Azure Service Bus, RabbitMQ, Kafka, and more (for the complete list, see the Dapr repository (*https://oreil.ly/Qnt8D*)).

Dapr uses Redis Streams as the default messaging backbone. The Stream is an append-only data structure introduced by Redis 5.0. You can use XADD to add data elements into a Stream, and you can use APIs like BLPOP to retrieve data. Each subscriber is assigned its own *consumer group* so that they can process their own copies of messages in parallel.

Dapr follows the CloudEvents v1.0 spec (*https://oreil.ly/f8tVe*). CloudEvents is a Cloud Native Computing Foundation (CNCF) sandbox-level project at the time of writing; its goal is to create a consistent way to describe events that can be used across event producers and consumers. Dapr implements all the required attributes: `id`, `source`, `specversion`, and `type`. It also implements the optional `datacontenttype` and `subject` attributes. Table 1-1 shows how these attributes are populated.

Table 1-1. CloudEvents attributes

Attribute	Value
`data`	Message payload
`datacontenttype`	`application/cloudevent+json`, `text/plain`, `application/json`
`id`	UUID
`source`	Sender Dapr ID
`specversion`	`1.0`
`subject`	Subscribed topic
`type`	`com.dapr.event.sent`

Dapr Components

Dapr groups different functionalities, such as pub/sub, the state store, middleware, and secrets, as components (a.k.a. building blocks). It ships with default implementations, but you can plug in alternate implementations if you like.

A component is defined by a metadata file, which is in the Kubernetes CRD format. For example, the following file defines a Redis state store named, quite creatively, `statestore`:

```
apiVersion: dapr.io/v1alpha1
kind: Component
metadata:
  name: statestore
spec:
  type: state.redis
  metadata:
  - name: redisHost
    value: <YOUR_REDIS_HOST_HERE>:6379
  - name: redisPassword
    value: <YOUR_REDIS_KEY_HERE>
```

When running in local mode, Dapr looks for a *./components* folder under your Dapr installation folder (which can be overridden by a `--component-path`) and loads all component files found under that folder. When running in Kubernetes mode, these files should be deployed to your Kubernetes cluster as CRDs. For example, to apply the preceding state store definition, you would use:

```
kubectl apply -f ./redis.yaml
```

The following is a definition of an OAuth 2.0 authorization middleware:

```
apiVersion: dapr.io/v1alpha1
kind: Component
metadata:
  name: oauth2
spec:
  type: middleware.http.oauth2
```

```
metadata:
- name: clientId
  value: "<your client ID>"
- name: clientSecret
  value: "<your client secret>"
- name: scopes
  value: "https://www.googleapis.com/auth/userinfo.email"
- name: authURL
  value: "https://accounts.google.com/o/oauth2/v2/auth"
- name: tokenURL
  value: "https://accounts.google.com/o/oauth2/token"
- name: redirectURL
  value: "http://dummy.com"
- name: authHeaderName
  value: "authorization"
```

This file defines a component of type `middleware.http.oauth2` named `oauth2`. You can assemble multiple middleware components into a custom pipeline by defining a custom configuration, as described next.

Dapr Configurations

A Dapr sidecar can be launched with a custom configuration, which is a file in local mode or a configuration object in Kubernetes mode. A Dapr configuration again uses Kubernetes CRD semantics so that the same configuration can be used in both local mode and Kubernetes mode.

At the time of writing, you can use Dapr configurations to customize distributed tracing and create custom pipelines. The schema is likely to be extended in future versions; consult the online Dapr documentation (*https://github.com/dapr/docs*) for updated details. The following sample shows a configuration that enables distributed tracing and defines a custom pipeline with the OAuth middleware:

```
apiVersion: dapr.io/v1alpha1
kind: Configuration
metadata:
  name: pipeline
spec:
  tracing:
    samplingRate: "1"
  httpPipeline:
    handlers:
    - type: middleware.http.oauth2
      name: oauth2
```

To apply this configuration, use `kubectl` (assuming the filename is *pipeline.yaml*):

```
kubectl apply -f ./pipeline.yaml
```

At the time of writing, you need to restart your pods to pick up new configuration changes.

To apply the custom configuration, you need to add a `dapr.io/config` annotation to your pod spec:

```
apiVersion: apps/v1
kind: Deployment
metadata:
  name: echoapp
  labels:
    app: echo
spec:
  replicas: 1
  selector:
    matchLabels:
      app: echo
  template:
    metadata:
      labels:
        app: echo
      annotations:
        dapr.io/enabled: "true"
        dapr.io/id: "echoapp"
        dapr.io/port: "3000"
        dapr.io/config: "pipeline"
    spec:
      containers:
      - name: echo
        image: <your Docker image tag>
        ports:
        - containerPort: 3000
        imagePullPolicy: Always
```

Custom Pipelines

Middleware defined in a custom pipeline are applied in the order in which they appear in the custom configuration file on the request side and in the reverse order on the response side. A middleware implementation can choose to participate in the ingress pipe, egress pipe, or both, as shown in Figure 1-4.

In addition to custom middleware, Dapr always loads two middleware at the top of the chain: the distributed tracing middleware and the CORS middleware. We'll talk about distributed tracing in the next section. CORS is configured by a runtime switch, `allowed-origins`, that contains a list of comma-separated allowed request origins. This switch may get merged into the Dapr configuration in future versions.

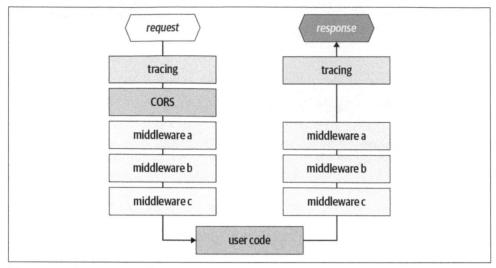

Figure 1-4. A custom pipeline

Custom Pipeline Experiment

In the following experiment, you'll create a custom pipeline with a strange middleware that changes all request bodies to uppercase. We created the middleware for testing purposes; you can use it to verify whether your custom pipeline is in place.

Since we've been using a different programing language for each of the samples so far, we'll switch to Rust for this exercise. You can certainly choose a different language and web framework to write the app, which simply echoes back what's received. The following discussion assumes you have Rust installed and configured on your machine.

Creating the Rust app

First, create the Rust app:

1. Create a new Rust project using `cargo`:

   ```
   cargo new rust-web
   cd rust-web
   ```

2. Modify your *Cargo.toml* file to include the necessary dependencies:

   ```
   [dependencies]
   actix-web = "2.0"
   actix-rt = "1.0.0"
   actix-service = "1.0.0"
   serde = "1.0"
   bytes = "0.5.2"
   json = "*"
   ```

3. Modify the *src/main.rs* file to contain the following code:

```
use actix_web::{
    web, App, Error, HttpResponse, HttpServer,
};
use json::JsonValue;
use bytes::{Bytes};

async fn echo(body: Bytes) -> Result<HttpResponse, Error> {
    let result = json::parse(std::str::from_utf8(&body).unwrap());
    // return result
    let injson: JsonValue = match result {
        Ok(v) => v,
        Err(e) => json::object! {"err" => e.to_string() },
    };
    Ok(HttpResponse::Ok()
        .content_type("application/json")
        .body(injson.dump()))
}

#[actix_rt::main]
async fn main() -> std::io::Result<()> {
    HttpServer::new(|| {
        App::new()
            .data(web::JsonConfig::default().limit(4096))
            .service(web::resource("/echo").route(web::post().to(echo)))
    })
    .bind("127.0.0.1:8088")?
    .run()
    .await
}
```

4. Launch the application and make sure it works:

```
cargo run
```

5. Use a web testing tool such as Postman to send a POST request to the web server with a JSON payload. You should see the payload played back in the response.

Define the custom pipeline

In this part of the exercise you'll create two manifest files, a Dapr configuration file and a middleware definition file:

1. Create a new *components* folder under your application folder.

2. Add a new *uppercase.yaml* file under this folder, with the following contents. The file defines a middleware.http.uppercase middleware, which doesn't have any metadata:

```
apiVersion: dapr.io/v1alpha1
kind: Component
```

```
metadata:
  name: uppercase
spec:
  type: middleware.http.uppercase
```

3. Define a *pipeline.yaml* file under your application folder with the following contents. This configuration defines a custom pipeline with a single `middle`
   `ware.http.uppercase` middleware:

```
apiVersion: dapr.io/v1alpha1
kind: Configuration
metadata:
  name: pipeline
spec:
  httpPipeline:
    handlers:
    - type: middleware.http.uppercase
      name: uppercase
```

Testing

To test the application locally, launch the Rust application with a Dapr sidecar from
your application folder:

```
dapr run --app-id rust-web --app-port 8088 --port 8080 --config ./pipeline.yaml
cargo run
```

Then use Postman to send a POST request to the following address with a JSON payload:

> *http://localhost:8080/v1.0/invoke/rust-web/method/echo*

You should see that the response JSON document contains only uppercase letters.

 Testing on Kubernetes is left as an exercise for interested readers.

OAuth 2.0 Authorization

OAuth 2.0 authorization middleware is one of the middleware components shipped
with Dapr. It enables the OAuth 2.0 Authorization Code Grant Flow. Specifically,
when a request is received by the Dapr sidecar with OAuth 2.0 middleware enabled,
the following steps happen:

1. The Dapr sidecar checks whether an authorization token exists. If not, Dapr redirects the browser to the configured authorization server.

2. The user logs in and grants access to the application. The request is redirected back to the Dapr sidecar with an authorization code.

3. Dapr exchanges the authorization code for an access token.

4. The sidecar injects the token into a configured header and forwards the request to the user application.

 At the time of writing, the middleware doesn't support refresh tokens.

Figure 1-5 illustrates how the OAuth middleware can be configured to provide OAuth authorization to an application.

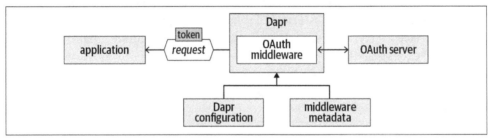

Figure 1-5. Custom pipeline with OAuth middleware

OAuth is a popular protocol that is supported by many authorization servers, including Azure AAD, Facebook, Fitbit, GitHub, Google APIs, Slack, Twitter, and more. To work with these authorization servers, you need to register your application with the servers you want to use. Different servers offer different registration experiences. At the end, you need to collect the following pieces of information:

- Client ID (*https://oreil.ly/FxaIz*)
- Client secret
- Scopes (*https://oreil.ly/C_Y9i*)
- Authorization URL
- Token URL

Table 1-2 lists the authorization and token URLs of some of the popular authorization servers.

Table 1-2. URLs of some authorization servers

Server	Authorization URL	Token URL
Azure AAD	*https://oreil.ly/M_5KZ*	*https://oreil.ly/3p0-u*
GitHub	*https://oreil.ly/tbgaL*	*https://oreil.ly/N2a_1*
Google APIs	*https://oreil.ly/H79ez*	*https://oreil.ly/zN1NP https://oreil.ly/SerId*
Twitter	*https://oreil.ly/FJKKk*	*https://oreil.ly/WtvKZ*

Once you collect the required information, you can define the OAuth middleware and your custom pipeline. The middleware follows the OAuth flow and injects the access token into the configured `authHeaderName` header.

Authoring a Custom Middleware

Dapr's HTTP server uses FastHTTP (*https://oreil.ly/WtvKZ*), so Dapr HTTP middleware are also written as FastHTTP handlers. Dapr defines a simple middleware interface that consists of one `GetHandler` method that returns a `fasthttp.RequestHandler`:

```
type Middleware interface {
  GetHandler(metadata Metadata) (func(h fasthttp.RequestHandler)
    fasthttp.RequestHandler, error)
}
```

Your implementation should return a function that takes in the downstream request handler and returns a new request handler. Then you can insert inbound or outbound logic around the downstream handler, as shown in the following code snippet:

```
func GetHandler(metadata Metadata) fasthttp.RequestHandler {
  return func(h fasthttp.RequestHandler) fasthttp.RequestHandler {
    return func(ctx *fasthttp.RequestCtx) {
      //inbound logic
      h(ctx)  //call the downstream handler
      //outbound logic
    }
  }
}
```

Your custom middleware, like other custom components, should be contributed to Dapr's *components-contrib* repository (*https://oreil.ly/CK1w8*), under the */middleware* folder. Then you'll need to submit another pull request against the main repository (*https://oreil.ly/juaoF*) to register the new middleware type. You'll also need to follow the registration process (*https://oreil.ly/zEK_E*) to register your middleware.

The registration process described here is likely to be eliminated in future versions. At the time of writing only HTTP middleware is supported, but we plan to support gRPC middleware in future versions as well.

Distributed Tracing

Diagnosing problems in a distributed application is challenging. You need to collect traces from multiple services and establish correlations among the log entries to establish the complete call chain. It's a daunting task, especially in a large-scale system with tens or even hundreds of services with millions of transactions every second.

Dapr makes your application topology more complex because it inserts sidecars around all participating services. On the other hand, because Dapr injects sidecars, it can provide help with diagnostics. Since all traffic flows through Dapr sidecars, Dapr can automatically establish correlations among requests and collect distributed traces into one consistent view. Dapr leverages OpenTelemetry (*https://oreil.ly/7eqRA*) to achieve this.

Another benefit of using Dapr distributed tracing is that your service code doesn't need to be instrumented, or to include any tracing libraries. All method calls are automatically traced by Dapr. And because tracing configuration is completely separate, changing or reconfiguring the tracing system doesn't affect your running applications. At the time of writing, Dapr doesn't expose a tracing API to user services for additional tracing needs. However, exposing such an API in Dapr has been discussed.

Tracing Middleware

Dapr distributed tracing is a middleware that can be plugged into any Dapr sidecar. It works under both the HTTP and gRPC protocols. The middleware is built around two key concepts: the span and correlation ID.

Span

A span represents a single operation, such as an HTTP request or a gRPC call. A span may have a *parent span* and multiple *child spans*. A span without a parent is called a *root span*. A span is identified by a *span ID*. Dapr keeps track of two kinds of spans: *server spans* and *client spans*. When a service receives a request, Dapr creates a server span. When a service invokes another service, Dapr creates a client span. The span types help tracing systems to track different roles in a service invocation.

Dapr extracts the method name from the request path and uses it as the span name, and it uses the span *status* to record the call result. Dapr maps HTTP response codes to a few span statuses, as summarized in Table 1-3.

Table 1-3. Span status mapping

HTTP response code	Span status
200	OK
201	OK
400	Invalid Argument
403	Permission Denied
404	Not Found
500	Internal
Other	Record as is

Correlation ID

Dapr uses a correlation ID to track a call chain across multiple services. When a request comes in Dapr searches for an X-Correlation-ID header in the HTTP request headers or gRPC metadata. If the ID exists, Dapr chains new tracing spans to the existing correlation ID. If not, Dapr considers the request a new client-initiated request and starts a new call chain.

Exporters

At the time of writing, Dapr uses OpenCensus (*https://opencensus.io*), which is getting merged into OpenTelemetry, for collecting distributed traces. OpenCensus supports the concept of *exporters*, which send traces and metrics to different tracing backends. Exporters are the extension points of OpenCensus, and they are what Dapr uses to connect to different backend systems such as Zipkin and Azure Monitor. At the time of writing, Dapr supports the OpenTelemetry native exporter, a Zipkin exporter, and a string exporter for testing purposes.

Configuration

Exporters are defined as Dapr components, and you can configure the overall tracing behavior with a Dapr configuration.

Tracing with Zipkin

Zipkin (*https://zipkin.io*) is a popular distributed tracing system. The following walk-through shows you the steps for configuring Dapr distributed tracing with Zipkin.

Creating configuration files

You need to define two artifacts, a Zipkin exporter component and a Dapr configuration with tracing enabled:

1. Create a *zipkin.yaml* file. Each exporter component has an enabled attribute that can be used to turn the exporter on or off. Other attributes are specific to the

exporter. The Zipkin exporter requires a single `exporterAddress` attribute, which points to the Zipkin API endpoint:

```
apiVersion: dapr.io/v1alpha1
kind: Component
metadata:
  name: zipkin
spec:
  type: exporters.zipkin
  metadata:
  - name: enabled
    value: "true"
  - name: exporterAddress
    value: "http://zipkin.default.svc.cluster.local:9411/api/v2/spans"
```

2. Create a Dapr configuration file named *tracing.yaml*. The configuration contains a `samplingRate` switch that controls how often the traces should be sampled (setting this to `"0"` disables tracing):

```
apiVersion: dapr.io/v1alpha1
kind: Configuration
metadata:
  name: tracing
spec:
  tracing:
    samplingRate: "1"
```

Deploying a Zipkin instance

Use the following command to deploy a Zipkin instance locally using a Docker container:

```
docker run -d -p 9411:9411 openzipkin/zipkin
```

To deploy a Zipkin instance on your Kubernetes cluster, use these commands:

```
kubectl run zipkin --image openzipkin/zipkin --port 9411
kubectl expose deploy zipkin --type ClusterIP --port 9411
```

Enabling and viewing tracing on Kubernetes

Follow these steps to enable tracing on Kubernetes:

1. Apply the exporter component and the Dapr configuration:

```
kubectl apply -f tracing.yaml
kubectl apply -f zipkin.yaml
```

2. Modify your pod spec to include an annotation that uses a custom Dapr configuration:

```
annotations:
  dapr.io/config: "tracing"
```

3. Deploy or restart your pod, and operate your service as usual. Traces are automatically collected and sent to the Zipkin endpoint.

4. You can use the Zipkin UI to view tracing data. To access the UI, you can set up port forwarding through kubectl, then use *http://localhost:9411* to view the tracing data:

```
kubectl port-forward svc/zipkin 9411:9411
```

Enabling and viewing tracing locally

To enable tracing locally, follow these steps:

1. Launch a local Zipkin instance as a Docker container:

```
docker run -d -p 9411:9411 openzipkin/zipkin
```

2. Modify the *zipkin.yaml* file to point to the local Zipkin endpoint:

```
apiVersion: dapr.io/v1alpha1
kind: Component
metadata:
  name: zipkin
spec:
  type: exporters.zipkin
  metadata:
  - name: enabled
    value: "true"
  - name: exporterAddress
    value: "http://localhost:9411/api/v2/spans"
```

3. Create a *components* folder under your application folder and move the *zipkin.yaml* file into that folder.

4. Launch your service with a Dapr sidecar using the following command:

```
dapr run --app-id mynode --app-port 3000 --config ./tracing.yaml
    <command to launch your service>
```

5. Use your service as usual. You can then view tracing data using the Zipkin UI at *http://localhost:9411*.

Tracing with Azure Monitor

At the time of writing, Dapr users a Local Forwarder (*https://oreil.ly/AnFOA*) that collects OpenCensus traces and telemetry data and forwards it to Application Insights. Dapr offers a prebuilt container, daprio/dapr-localforwarder, to facilitate the configuration process. Once you have the container running, you can follow steps similar to those used to configure Zipkin to configure the Local Forwarder as a ClusterIP service on your Kubernetes cluster. Once the Local Forwarder is configured, enter the Local Forwarder agent endpoint in your native exporter configuration file:

```
apiVersion: dapr.io/v1alpha1
kind: Component
metadata:
  name: native
spec:
  type: exporters.native
  metadata:
  - name: enabled
    value: "true"
  - name: agentEndpoint
    value: "<Local Forwarder address, for example: 50.140.60.170:6789>"
```

You can then use the rich Azure Monitor features to view and analyze your collected tracing data. Figure 1-6 shows an example of the Azure Monitor UI showing an application with multiple services calling each other.

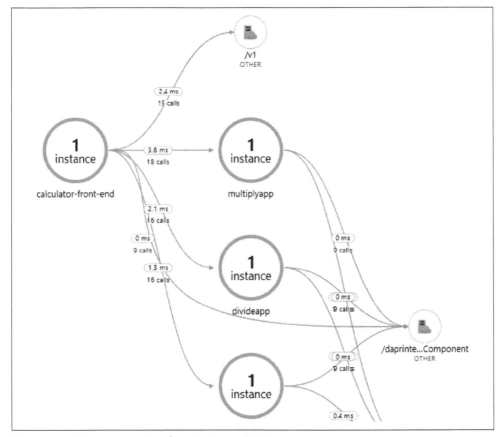

Figure 1-6. Viewing tracing data in Azure Monitor

You can deploy multiple exporters at the same time. Dapr forwards traces to all exporters.

Service Operation

As a distributed programming model and runtime, Dapr doesn't concern itself with service operation. However, Dapr is designed to work with existing Kubernetes toolchains and new open source projects such as OAM for managing applications that are comprised of multiple services. This section is not meant to provide a comprehensive introduction, but to be an index of related resources.

Service Deployment and Upgrade

When running on Kubernetes, Dapr uses the sidecar injector that automatically injects Dapr sidecar containers into pods annotated with the `dapr.io/enabled` attribute. You then manage your pods as usual using common Kubernetes tools such as `kubectl`. For example, the following YAML file describes a deployment with a single container and a load-balanced service (this example is from the distributed calculator sample which you can find in Dapr's sample repository (*https://oreil.ly/M2bEP*)):

```
kind: Service
apiVersion: v1
metadata:
  name: calculator-front-end
  labels:
    app: calculator-front-end
spec:
  selector:
    app: calculator-front-end
  ports:
  - protocol: TCP
    port: 80
    targetPort: 8080
  type: LoadBalancer

---
apiVersion: apps/v1
kind: Deployment
metadata:
  name: calculator-front-end
  labels:
    app: calculator-front-end
spec:
  replicas: 1
  selector:
    matchLabels:
      app: calculator-front-end
  template:
    metadata:
      labels:
        app: calculator-front-end
      annotations:
```

```
      dapr.io/enabled: "true"
      dapr.io/id: "calculator-front-end"
      dapr.io/port: "8080"
  spec:
    containers:
    - name: calculator-front-end
      image: dapriosamples/distributed-calculator-react-calculator
      ports:
      - containerPort: 8080
      imagePullPolicy: Always
```

You can use kubectl to deploy the deployment:

```
kubectl apply -f calculator-front-end.yaml
```

Once the deployment is created, you can use kubectl to scale it to multiple replicas:

```
kubectl scale deployment calculator-front-end --replicas=3
```

You can also use kubectl to update a deployment to a new image version—for example:

```
kubectl set image deployment.v1.apps/calculator-front-end calculator-front-end
  =dapriosamples/distributed-calculator-react-calculator:<version tag>
```

> For more information on managing Kubernetes deployments, consult the documentation (*https://oreil.ly/t3VLX*).

OAM

Open Application Model (*https://oam.dev*) is an open source project that aims to provide a platform-agnostic modeling language for cloud native applications. OAM describes the topology of an *application* that is comprised of multiple interconnected *components*. It is concerned with application topology, but not with how individual services are written. Dapr goes to a deeper level and provides a common programming model and the supporting runtime for cloud native applications. As you've seen earlier in this chapter, Dapr can handle service name resolution and invocation routing. At the same time, Dapr can be configured to be used with existing service mesh systems to provide fine-tuned traffic control among services. Figure 1-7 shows how OAM's logical topology, Dapr routes, and service mesh policies overlay on top of each other.

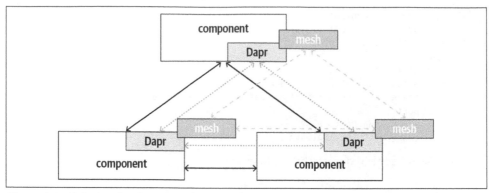

Figure 1-7. Relationship between OAM and Dapr

OAM allows you to attach *traits* to each component to control behavior such as scaling. For example, the following manual scaling trait scales a `frontend` component to five replicas:

```
apiVersion: core.oam.dev/v1alpha1
kind: ApplicationConfiguration
metadata:
  name: custom-single-app
  annotations:
    version: v1.0.0
    description: "Customized version of single-app"
spec:
  variables:
  components:
    - componentName: frontend
      instanceName: web-front-end
      parameterValues:
      traits:
        - name: ManualScaler
          properties:
            replicaCount: 5
```

You can group multiple components into a *scope,* and you can associate scopes, components, and traits through an *application configuration.* The core rationale behind this design is separation of concerns. The goal of OAM is to give developers a way to describe an application independently of any infrastructural concerns, to give the application operators a way to configure applications to satisfy business needs, and to give the infrastructural operators a way to describe how the desired topology and configuration are realized on a specific platform.

A common form of component is a container deployed as a Kubernetes pod. This means you can add Dapr annotations to your component and the Dapr sidecar injector can inject Dapr sidecars into your pods.

The combination of OAM and Dapr provides a complete solution for writing platform-agnostic applications—OAM provides the platform-agnostic modeling language, and Dapr provides abstract common APIs for state, service invocation, pub/sub, security, and bindings. At the time of writing, both OAM and Dapr are under active development. It's expected that more integrations will be introduced in future versions.

Why do we believe writing platform-agnostic applications is important? Because we envision a future of ubiquitous computing, in which compute happens within the context of data. An application should be adaptive to where data is. This means applications need to work on different cloud platforms and on-premises systems, as well as in hybrid environments that span across cloud and edge.

Summary

This chapter provided a detailed introduction to how Dapr enables services to communicate with each other through direct invocations as well as messaging. You also saw how Dapr allows the construction of customized processing pipelines through middleware. You can chain multiple middleware together to form a custom pipeline that can intercept and transform either ingress traffic or egress traffic.

Dapr offers built-in support for distributed tracing over both the HTTP and gRPC protocols. Distributed tracing is a mandatory feature of a distributed framework to efficiently diagnose a distributed application. Dapr leverages OpenTelemetry to integrate with various tracing backends.

OAM and Dapr aim at providing a complete solution for writing platform-agnostic cloud native applications. OAM provides a platform-agnostic modeling language to describe application topology. Dapr provides HTTP/gRPC-based APIs that abstract common tasks such as service name resolution and invocation, pub/sub, state management, security management, and bindings to external services.

In the next chapter, we'll introduce the Dapr state API.

CHAPTER 2

State

State management is an important topic in application design. From file access to relational databases to key/value stores, most applications need to manipulate state one way or another. State management in the cloud brings its own unique challenges, as we'll discuss in this chapter. Dapr state management aims to provide a simple state API that helps you deal with these challenges while writing clean, platform-agnostic state-handling code.

State Management

Calling a customer service line can be a painful experience—you wait on the line for tens of minutes, you spend more time explaining your situation, you dodge all the playbook moves designed to keep you from canceling your order or subscription, and then the call disconnects. After another long wait, you finally get reconnected, and then you need to start all over again with a new agent.

Some customer service departments first open a case when you call. If the call gets disconnected, you can then reconnect and pick up where you left off, because the new agent will have some context of what happened in the previous call. It's often still a tedious experience, but being able to resume rather than starting over is definitely an improvement.

The support case number serves as an enduring record during a complex transaction. When the transaction is handled by multiple agents, the transaction state is carried over by the case number. This is the behavior of a stateful service, which is the focus of the chapter.

Stateless Versus Stateful

Web services can be put into two broad categories: stateless and stateful. A stateless service doesn't maintain contextual information between requests. For example, a search through a search engine is an independent request. All the search engine needs is the search pattern; it doesn't need any additional contextual information to carry out the search. If you get disconnected after you issue the search, you need to resubmit the search query when you get reconnected, because the search engine doesn't remember your previous searches.

A stateful service maintains contextual information during a transaction, which may span multiple requests. For example, as you add items to your online shopping cart, the web server keeps track of the items in your cart so that you can keep shopping and check out all the items later.

Another way to distinguish a stateful service from a stateless service is where the state is saved. A service that keeps state is not necessarily a stateful service. For example, consider a student record management system that updates a database of student records. Each CRUD (Create, Read, Update, Delete) operation is an independent request; if an operation fails halfway through, you need to resubmit the request. However, if the service maintains contextual information on the compute node itself, it becomes stateful.

In the rest of the chapter, we'll treat services that save state on compute nodes as stateful services. We use this definition because hosting a service with local state on compute nodes is quite different from hosting a stateless service.

Why Are Stateless Services Preferred in the Cloud?

Many cloud platforms have a strong preference for stateless services. This is because stateless services fit naturally with the characteristics of cloud computing.

Scaling a stateless service

A search engine is backed by thousands of backend servers. When a request is issued, it goes through a load balancer and gets routed to any one of those servers. It doesn't matter which server ends up handling the request, because everything needed to handle the request is carried by the request itself. Having multiple servers to share the workload is called *scaling out*, and this is the main means of scaling in the cloud.

On-premises systems often scale by *scaling up*, which involves increasing the capacity of existing servers to match the increased workload.

There's no theoretical limit to scaling out in cloud computing. You can scale to thousands of servers if you need (and can afford) to, and you can *scale in* when you no longer need that many servers anymore. Being able to scale in and out at any time is referred to as *elasticity*, and it's one of the biggest value propositions of cloud versus on-premises datacenters.

Stateless services can often take advantage of multiple levels of caching, such as content delivery network (CDN) and server-side caches. Going back to the search engine example, a search engine can cache the results of popular searches so it doesn't need to go back to the backend database to retrieve them. For a read-heavy system, caching can tremendously boost scalability and performance.

Stateless service availability

Cloud platforms use commodity servers, which have a higher probability of failure than the high-end servers you might have in your on-premises datacenters. Because of the sheer number of servers in the cloud, some will fail merely by probability—and the failing servers could be the ones that handle your workload. Therefore, people say that in cloud, failure is the norm and you have to embrace failures. The easiest way to deal with such failures is to have backups.

Servers behind a load balancer serve as backups of each other. When a server fails, it's taken off the load balancer to be repaired, while other servers continue to serve user requests. When you add a new server behind a load balancer, you effectively add another "9" to your service availability. Assume that you have two identical servers, each with an availability of 90%. Joining them behind a load balancer gives you 99% availability, and adding a third server gives you 99.9% availability.

Serverless

Since it doesn't matter which physical server ends up handling a request, as an application writer, you don't need to care where and how those servers are hosted. If you can be guaranteed to have the required compute and storage capacity at any time, you don't need to worry about the underlying infrastructure at all—hence the serverless promise. To deliver that promise in a sustainable manner, a cloud platform needs to efficiently distribute workloads across its available resources. Scheduling a stateless service is much easier than scheduling a stateful service, as we'll see in a moment. Therefore, many serverless platforms support only stateless services.

Challenges of Hosting Stateful Services

Hosting stateful services presents several practical challenges. Because a stateful service holds contextual information during a transaction that may span multiple requests, all requests within a transaction need to be handled only by the servers that hold that contextual state to ensure consistency. This constraint introduces extra complexity to workload scheduling, making hosting stateful services at scale a much more difficult task.

Stateful service availability

When a server fails, it loses the contextual information it holds in memory. Even if the server holds the state on its local disk, when it fails, other servers won't be able to retrieve state from it. To ensure stateful service availability, the state needs to be replicated to multiple servers so that when one server fails, other servers can continue with the transaction using their own copies of the state.

To implement such state replication, we need to solve a few problems. First, we need to come up with a strategy to pick servers to participate in the replication. A common practice is to pick a number of servers to form a *replica set*. As long as a quorum in the replica set (often an odd-numbered subset) has consensus on what the state consists of, the state is available. When we make choices, we must consider the load on these servers to avoid overloading certain servers. We may also want to ensure these servers are sufficiently far apart (such as on different server racks, or in different *failure domains*) that they are unlikely to fail together. After we've made the initial choice, we still need to implement additional mechanisms to dynamically adjust our choices. For example, when a replica set's size falls below the minimum required quorum size because too many servers become unavailable, we need to recruit new servers and join them to the replica set.

Second, we need to decide on a replication strategy. If we use a *strong consistency* model, every state update needs to be confirmed by the quorum members before it's committed. This slows down the system. Alternatively, we can use an *eventual consistency* model, in which replication happens asynchronously. In such a model, user requests are routed to a *primary* server, whose state server is periodically replicated to *secondary* servers. If the primary fails, a secondary is promoted to the position of primary. Because state replication is asynchronous, when the primary fails any requests that are in flight will be lost, and the system state will be reverted to a previous state, measured by recovery point objective (RPO). Selecting a single primary without a centralized coordinator is tricky. When multiple members are accidentally selected as primaries at the same time (due to network partition, for instance), we have a "split brain" situation that can lead to problems such as state corruption.

Last but not least, as the servers will be serving multiple tenants and multiple concurrent transactions at the same time, we have to ensure these transactions are isolated from each other for reasons of both security and performance. For example, replication of transactions should be done independently so that a complex transaction doesn't slow down other transactions. Also, a tenant should never be able to peek at transactions from other tenants, either accidentally or intentionally. This requires fine granular access control over state data, down to the transaction level.

It should now be obvious that ensuring stateful service availability is a much more complex problem than ensuring the availability of stateless services. As a matter of fact, efficient state replication and leader election are among the most difficult distributed computing problems.

Scaling stateful services

Unlike stateless services, stateful services require all requests in a transaction to be routed to the same replica set. Hence, a load balancer for stateful services can't blindly distribute requests to all available servers. Instead, it must remember which requests belong to which replica sets. When a stateful service is being scaled out, it's often segmented into *partitions*. A replica set is constrained to a single partition. When the system needs to recruit a new server for a replica set, it searches among servers only in the same partition. This makes managing replica sets more efficient, especially in large clusters.

We can choose from a number of partitioning strategies, both static and dynamic. Partitioning by region ID is an example of static partitioning, and partitioning by consistent hash is an example of dynamic partitioning. Dynamic partitions can be adjusted as the number of available servers changes. When a new server joins the cluster, the partitions are redistributed to leverage the additional capacity; when the cluster shrinks, partitions are compacted into the remaining resources.

When partitioning is used, the partition ID can be factored into the request path to assist in routing. For example, the request path to a partitioned foo service may look like:

> *https://<host>/<partition>/foo*

This routing scheme requires the load balancer to support routing by partitions. If the load balancer doesn't support partitioned routing, an extra hop may occur. For example, if a request intended for partition A is routed to a partition B server, that server needs to forward the request to a partition A server.

Workloads on partitions may become imbalanced. As some busy partitions are overwhelmed by requests, other idle partitions remain dormant, wasting compute resources. Some advanced schedulers support *resource balancing*, which dynamically rearranges partitions on server nodes so that the servers are evenly loaded. Moving a partition around is expensive, though, because it must carry its state data with it. So the scheduler has to find a balance between reducing the number of moves and keeping resource consumption balanced across servers.

The point is, scaling stateful services is also hard.

Converting Stateful Services to Stateless Services

It's simple to convert a stateful service to a stateless service—you just need to externalize the state to a separate data store, such as a replicated database. Using external state stores has a detrimental impact on system performance, because all state operations become remote calls, which are orders of magnitude slower than local state operations. However, with modern networking, such delays are often tolerable unless the system is extremely sensitive to the increased response time.

Figure 2-1 illustrates how a stateful service is converted into a stateless service by externalizing its state. On the left is a stateful service consisting of three instances. Each instance commits state locally, and the state is replicated and reconciled across the cluster. On the right, the state is moved into an external state store, which is replicated to multiple replicas for high availability. The instances may hold local caches to improve performance, with different cache update policies such as *write-through*, *write-around*, and *write-back*.

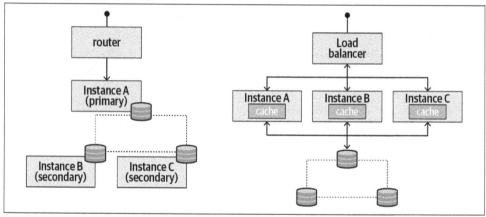

Figure 2-1. Stateful service (left) versus stateless service with state (right)

The architecture on the right is more complicated and often less performant than the architecture on the left. However, a key benefit of the design is that the service instances become stateless and thus are much easier to manage in the cloud.

Dapr State Management

Dapr brings state management to services through a reliable state endpoint. This allows transforming stateful services into stateless services, which as we've seen are much easier to manage. Developers can save and retrieve state through a simple Dapr state API. Dapr supports a pluggable architecture that allows user services to be bound to different state stores, such as Redis, Azure Cosmos DB, Cassandra, AWS DynamoDB, and Google Cloud Spanner.

Concurrency Model

Dapr-compatible state stores are required to support optimistic concurrency using *ETags*. When a state item is retrieved, it's associated with an ETag. When a service instance tries to update the state item, the newly updated state item has to bear the same ETag in the data store. Optimistic concurrency assumes that most updates to a state store can be carried out independently from one another, as there's often a single mutator of a specific state item. When multiple service instances try to update the same state item, the first writer will win because it holds the matching ETag. Other update attempts will fail, and those service instances will need to retrieve the latest state and try again. If a client omits the ETag, the state store is supposed to revert to *last-write-wins*, which means the last received write request supersedes previous requests.

Consistency Model

Dapr requires state stores to support eventual consistency by default. A state store can also opt to support strongly consistent writes. For example, the default Dapr Redis state store implementation uses eventual consistency. However, if a client sends a request with the strong consistency flag, Dapr waits until all replicas have acknowledged the write request before it turns to the caller.

To write applications that are intended to work with multiple data stores, you should assume the state stores support eventual consistency. Some frameworks prefer strong consistency, as strong consistency is easier to reason with. However, we believe eventual consistency is more natural to a distributed system, and it has been broadly adopted. Hence, Dapr chooses eventual consistency as the default behavior.

Bulk Operations and Transactions

Dapr requires data stores to ensure transactional isolation for a single insert, update, or delete operation. The Dapr state API also defines bulk read, bulk delete, and bulk update operations, but it doesn't mandate that these operations be handled as a single transaction.

Dapr defines a separate transactional store interface, which supports handling multiple database operations as isolated transactions. A store supporting the transactional store interface is called a *transactional state store*. A transactional state store is required to support the actor programming model (see Chapter 5 for details).

Multiple State Stores

Dapr supports multiple state stores on the same cluster. Each store is identified by a store name and is configured as a Dapr component. For example, when you write a digital music library, you can save album information into Cosmos DB and keep the

actual audio files in blob storage. At the time of writing, Dapr doesn't support transactions across multiple state stores. Your application should use a single state store as
a single source of truth and use other stores to save associated data.

Retry Policies

Dapr ships with a simple retry library that automatically retries failed operations
based on either a *linear* retry policy or an *exponential backoff* retry policy. A retry policy contains an interval and a maximum threshold. A data operation is retried at the
given interval until the maximum retry threshold is reached. A linear retry policy has
fixed intervals. An exponential backoff policy has exponentially increasing intervals,
defined as $interval_i = initial\ interval \times 2^i$, where $interval_i$ is the interval after the *i*th
try of the data operation.

The Dapr State API

Dapr defines a simple state API based on a key/value paradigm, as shown in the following code snippet:

```
type Store interface {
    Init(metadata Metadata) error
    Delete(req *DeleteRequest) error
    BulkDelete(req []DeleteRequest) error
    Get(req *GetRequest) (*GetResponse, error)
    Set(req *SetRequest) error
    BulkSet(req []SetRequest) error
}
```

A transaction state store implements an additional `TransactionalStore` interface:

```
type TransactionalStore interface {
    Init(metadata Metadata) error
    Multi(reqs []TransactionalRequest) error
}
```

You can attach additional options to each request. Dapr defines a few predefined
attributes for each operation. It also allows a key/value map to be attached to a
request, which it passes to the underlying data store as is. This design allows a data
store to offer additional features on top of the basic API. However, when you leverage
store-specific attributes, your code is less portable across different state stores.

Dapr requires data stores to honor the attached operations on a best-attempt basis.
Hence, using any of the additional options may impact the portability of your application. You should consult the stores' implementation details to make your choices.

Key Scheme

All state stores are expected to follow the same key scheme. For general states, the key format is *<Dapr ID>||<state key>*. For actor states, the key format is *<App ID>|| <Actor type>||<Actor ID>||<state key>*. When you invoke Dapr state APIs, you supply the state key. Dapr automatically prepends the Dapr ID. For example, a state request sent to Dapr ID `dapr1` with state key `mystate` uses `dapr1||mystate` as the actual key to access the underlying state store.

Get Requests

A Get request has a `consistency` option whose value can be either `eventual` or `strong`. Some state stores, such as Azure Cosmos DB, support consistent read, which means any read from any database service is guaranteed to reflect the latest committed write.

The Dapr state store returns a response with a `Data` attribute and an `ETag` attribute. The former contains the actual data, and the latter contains the corresponding ETag. Dapr doesn't define a canonical ETag format. When you migrate a data element from one store to another, you should treat writing to the second store as a new Set request without the ETag.

Dapr returns a 204 response if the requested key is not found. It returns 400 if the state store is missing or misconfigured, and 500 for any other unexpected errors from the database server.

To send a Get request through Dapr, you send a GET request to *http://local:<Dapr port>/v1.0/state/<state store name>/<key>*—for example: *http://localhost:3600/v1.0/ state/mystatestore/key-1*.[1]

Set Requests

A Set request consists of the following fields:

key
: The key of the value to be updated.

value
: The new data value.

etag
: The known ETag associated with the value. This ETag was returned from a previous Get request.

---

[1] At the time of writing, a new bulk get API is being added to allow retrieving multiple keys in a single request.

```
options
```

The options include:

```
concurrency
    first-write or last-write
```

```
consistency
    eventual or strong
```

```
retryPolicy
```
A retry policy that consists of an `interval`, a `threshold`, and a `pattern`, which can be either `linear` or `exponential`

 You might have noticed that Dapr doesn't define an *insert* operation. This is because in a distributed system, every insert operation should be an *upsert* operation, which performs a transactional insert or update based on whether the given key exists.

You can perform bulk set operations through the `BulkSet` method. As explained before, the bulk operation is not handled as an isolated transaction, which means it may partially succeed. You can attach a retry policy to a bulk operation, though.

To send a Set request through Dapr, POST a JSON array of key/value pairs to *http://localhost:<Dapr port>/v1.0/state/<state store name>*.

Delete Requests

Delete requests and bulk delete requests are similar to Set requests, except for the `concurrency` option, which isn't relevant in this case.

To send a Delete request through Dapr, send a DELETE request to *http://localhost:<Dapr port>/v1.0/state/<state store name>/<key>*. The request header optionally contains an `If-Match` header that contains the known ETag.

Transactional Requests

You can submit transactional requests to transactional state stores. The request is a list of upsert operations or delete operations. All operations in a transactional request succeed or fail as a whole—either all operations are carried out, or none of the operations are performed. At the time of writing, you can't attach a retry policy to a transactional request.

Working with the Dapr State API

Working with the Dapr state API is straightforward, as shown in the following Node.js sample code that updates an `order` state:

```
const state = [{
  key: "order",
  value: data
}];
fetch("http://localhost:3500/v1.0/state/statestore", {
  method: "POST",
  body: JSON.stringify(state),
  headers: {
    "Content-Type": "application/json"
  }
}).then((response) => {
  if (!response.ok) {
    throw "Failed to persist state.";
  }
});
```

Figure 2-2 shows the data flow of using the Dapr state API. Reading and setting state is accomplished via simple HTTP calls through the Dapr endpoint.

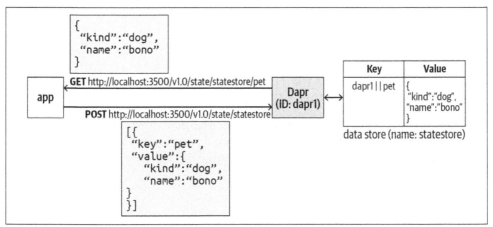

Figure 2-2. Working with the Dapr state API

The Dapr state API is a very simple key/value-oriented API. We (and the community) have made some choices about including or excluding features based on feedback and customer requirements. This section covers a few features that are not offered by the Dapr state API out of the box but can be implemented through alternative means.

Data Handling Considerations

Dapr doesn't perform data transformation, encryption, or compression out of the box. You have two choices to achieve these: through a custom data store implementation or through a custom middleware. The custom middleware is likely to be the better option because it can perform consistent operations across different data stores—and chances are that by the time you're reading this some such middleware implementations are already available. One thing to be aware of is that in this case your custom middleware should respond only to state-related routes.

 Since a middleware is a Dapr component, you can use secret references in your middleware description file. This allows you to safely store your secrets such as encryption keys in your preferred secret stores. We'll discuss security in more detail in Chapter 4.

Dapr doesn't limit data sizes. However, each data store has its own limits and constraints on the data it stores. A data store may also impose rate limits on the number of requests per time unit. Dapr doesn't handle these differences. It's up to the developer to adapt to the constraints of specific data stores.

Dapr uses a simple string key. To support partitions, you can configure multiple state stores, each pointing at a different partition. For example, you can configure different state store connections for different collections in Azure Cosmos DB, or different buckets in Amazon S3. Separate state stores are useful for static partitioning. For dynamic partitioning, you can use a custom store implementation or a custom middleware to implement your partitioning logic.

Dapr doesn't support partial updates to a value. The new value needs to be posted in its entirety in order to update any parts of it. You'll need to use a custom state store or middleware to support updating data by submitting deltas.

Data Querying and Aggregation

Many customers—especially IoT customers—have expressed the need to run flexible queries and aggregations across many keys. At the time of writing, we are still debating what kind of query API or aggregation API Dapr should offer.[2] However, a good thing about Dapr's state store design is that it doesn't use a proprietary state format. You can operate directly on the backend state stores to realize complex queries and aggregations.

---

2 Some discussed languages/protocols include T-SQL, oData and GraphQL, but the team hasn't settled on a direction at the time of this writing.

Read-only access to the backend store is generally safe. But mutating the data directly through the state store could be dangerous. Your code needs to maintain ETags in the same way that Dapr maintains ETags, or Dapr may get confused and reject legitimate update requests. It's recommended that you apply proper RBAC on the backend stores to avoid accidental updates from unauthorized applications or users.

State Stores

Dapr initially shipped with two state stores: Redis and Azure Cosmos DB. Since the original announcement, the community has contributed many other state stores, including:

- HashiCorp Consul
- Etcd
- Cassandra
- Memcached
- MongoDB
- ZooKeeper
- Google Cloud Firestore
- AWS DynamoDB
- Couchbase

At the time of writing, more state stores are being worked on. This section provides additional details on some of the available state stores. We hope this information is helpful when you try to implement your own Dapr-compatible state stores.

Redis

Redis is an in-memory data structure store. It provides an on-cluster storage solution with a great balance between performance and reliability, and it's easy to configure. This is why Redis is Dapr's default state store.

Dapr uses *hashes* instead of *sets* to save data. The primary reason for using hashes is to treat a data element and its associated ETag as a single unit. At the time of writing, Redis doesn't natively support ETags, so Dapr uses an ever-incrementing version number as the ETag. To ensure data element update and ETag maintenance are handled as a single transaction, Dapr uses Lua script (*https://www.lua.org*) to carry out all Set and Delete requests because Redis executes all commands in a Lua script in a single transaction. For example, the following Lua script is used to update a key:

```
local var1 = redis.pcall("HGET", KEYS[1], "version");
if type(var1) == "table" then
```

```
    redis.call("DEL", KEYS[1]);
end;
if not var1 or type(var1) == "table" or var1 == "" or
  var1 == ARGV[1] or ARGV[1] == "0" then
  redis.call("HSET", KEYS[1], "data", ARGV[2])
  return redis.call("HINCRBY", KEYS[1], "version", 1)
else
  return error("failed to set key " .. KEYS[1])
end
```

To query all states associated with the Dapr ID `myapp`, use this query:

```
KEYS myapp*
```

To get data from a specific key named `balance`, use the following query (note that you need to prefix the Dapr ID in this case):

```
HGET myapp||balance data
```

To get the associated ETag, use this:

```
HGET myapp||balance version
```

Azure Cosmos DB

Azure Cosmos DB is a globally distributed, multimodel database service. It supports operating on the same data set through multiple popular APIs, including SQL, MongoDB, Cassandra, Gremlin, and more.

Dapr uses Cosmos DB's SQL API to save state data. A Cosmos DB state store is configured for a specific *collection* on a Cosmos DB database. To use multiple collections, you need to define a separate state store for each.

To query all states associated with the Dapr ID `myapp`, use this SQL query (assuming the Cosmos DB collection is named `states`):

```
SELECT * FROM states WHERE CONTAINS(states.id, 'myapp||')
```

To get data from a specific key named `balance`, use the following query:

```
SELECT * FROM states WHERE states.id = 'myapp||balance'
```

To get the ETag, use the system `_etag` column:

```
SELECT states._etag FROM states WHERE states.id ='myapp||balance'
```

You can also use Cosmos DB's aggregation functions to perform more advanced queries. For example, the following query calculates the sum of all values in the `states` collection (assuming the data is saved in a `value` field):

```
SELECT VALUE SUM(s.value) FROM states s
```

In addition, you can use various data visualization and analysis tools that support Cosmos DB. For instance, you can use the Power BI Cosmos DB connector to import and visualize your state data in Power BI.

Because Cosmos DB is a globally distributed data store, you can leverage it to deploy globally distributed stateful services. For example, Figure 2-3 shows a service deployed in multiple Azure regions. The service instances are joined behind an Azure Traffic Manager to route users to different regions based on metrics such as proximity to the end user or the latency to the region. Because both Dapr instances share the same ID in this case, they can each read and write the data as if it were in a local regional database.

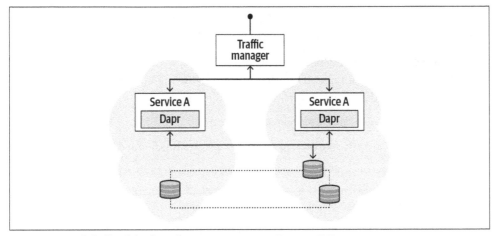

Figure 2-3. Globally distributed state store using Cosmos DB

Etcd

Etcd is a distributed, reliable key/value store. Kubernetes uses etcd as the native state store. Etcd maintains multiple revisions of values. Each stored key/value pair is immutable. Mutative operations on existing keys create new revisions. You can use revision numbers as ETags; however, when you write back a data element, because etcd doesn't reinforce the version check, you'll need to do this using the txn command, or in your client code—such as in the Dapr state store implementation. Because this check and the following mutation are not transactional without an additional locking mechanism and locking often has negative impacts on system performance, at the time of writing the accepted etcd store implementation doesn't perform ETag checks on updates, as shown in the following code:

```
func (r *ETCD) Set(req *state.SetRequest) error {
  ctx, cancelFn :=
    context.WithTimeout(context.Background(), r.operationTimeout)
  defer cancelFn()
  var vStr string
```

```
  b, ok := req.Value.([]byte)
  if ok {
    vStr = string(b)
  } else {
    vStr, _ = r.json.MarshalToString(req.Value)
  }
  _, err := r.client.Put(ctx, req.Key, vStr)
  if err != nil {
    return err
  }
  return nil
}
```

So, strictly speaking, the existing implementation isn't complete. This issue is tracked by issue number #169 (*https://oreil.ly/viyGa*) in the *components-contrib* repository. Check the issue status for updated details.

You can use etcd's command-line tool, `etcdctl`, to query your etcd store. To query all states associated with the Dapr ID `myapp`, use the following command (assuming `END POINTS` points to etcd host endpoints, separated by commas):

```
etcdctl --endpoints=$ENDPOINTS get myapp –prefix
```

To get data from a specific key named `balance`, use the following query:

```
etcdctl --endpoints=$ENDPOINTS get myapp||balance --print-value-only
```

Apache Cassandra

Cassandra is a scalable NoSQL database with high availability and reliability. It uses a peer-to-peer distributed system architecture, with each node being able to accept read and write requests. It uses a *gossip protocol* to keep data synchronized among the nodes.

Cassandra is a column-based database. The outermost container for data in Cassandra is called a *keyspace*. Within a keyspace you can define *column families* (a.k.a. *tables*), which are containers for ordered collections of *rows*. Each row, in turn, is an ordered collection of *columns*. In the current implementation, a Dapr state store maps to a specific table in your Cassandra database.

You can perform queries on a Cassandra database using the Cassandra Query Language (CQL). For example, to insert (or update) a row with a `key` column and a `value` column to a table, using the following query:

```
INSERT INTO mytable (key, value) VALUES ('myapp||balance', 1000)
```

To get the column back by the given key, use the following query:

```
SELECT value FROM mytable WHERE key = 'myapp||balance'
```

And to delete a row by a key, use:

```
DELETE FROM mytable WHERE key = 'myapp||balance'
```

Figure 2-4 shows a simplified data model of Cassandra and how entities are mapped into Dapr state API constructs in the previous examples.

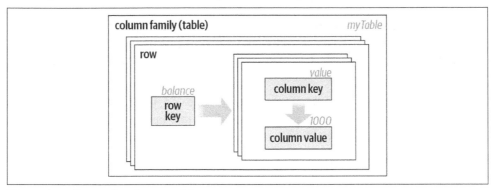

Figure 2-4. Cassandra data model

Couchbase

Couchbase is a NoSQL document database that supports a full REST API for managing JSON-based documents and custom views. It uses a data structure called Compare and Swap (CAS) to represent the current state of an item. CAS values work in the same way as ETags: if the user-supplied CAS value matches what's currently in the database, the mutation operation is allowed; otherwise the operation fails, and the user must try again with an up-to-date CAS value.

Couchbase organizes documents into buckets. A Dapr state store is associated with a specific Couchbase bucket. In addition to the REST API, Couchbase supports a query language named N1QL (pronounced "nickel"). For example, to query documents by ID, you would use a query like this:

```
SELECT * FROM bucket1 USE KEYS myapp||balance
```

You can use the N1QL ARRAY_AGG function to aggregate data across documents, or you can define a MapReduce *view* that contains a map function that projects documents to the desired shape and an optional reduce function that aggregates data together. For example, you can use a built-in _sum reduce function to calculate the sum of data values, which is equivalent to the following custom implementation:

```
function(key, values, rereduce) {
  var sum = 0;
  for(i=0; i < values.length; i++) {
    sum = sum + values[i];
  }
  return(sum);
}
```

Custom State Stores

Dapr state stores are Dapr components, which are described by component manifests as you've seen in previous chapters.

In case you haven't noticed, when you use the `dapr init` command, the Dapr CLI automatically creates a *components* folder with two YAML files: *redis.yaml*, which defines a default Redis-based state store, and *redis_messagebus.yaml*, which defines a pub/sub backbone using Redis Streams.

A state store definition contains a name, a type, and a collection of key/value pairs specifying connection information and the configurable options of the data store, as in the autogenerated *redis.yaml* file:

```
apiVersion: dapr.io/v1alpha1
kind: Component
metadata:
  name: statestore
spec:
  type: state.redis
  metadata:
  - name: redisHost
    value: localhost:6379
  - name: redisPassword
    value: ""
```

A custom state store is configured in the same way. To write a custom state store, you follow the general steps of writing a custom Dapr component:

1. Implement your custom component in the Dapr *components-contrib* repository.
2. Update the Dapr runtime to register your custom component type.
3. Create the manifest file for your component.
4. Deploy the manifest file to Kubernetes as a CRD definition when running on Kubernetes, or copy the file to the *components* folder when running locally.
5. Based on the custom component type, you may need to modify or create a custom Dapr configuration to use the component. You can skip this step for custom state stores, because Dapr automatically picks up custom state stores by their names.

Implementing the State API

Your custom state store should go under the *https://oreil.ly/TT-1v* folder. Create a separate folder for your state store. If you are working on a managed state store from a cloud platform such as Azure or GCP, you should put the custom store under the corresponding folder for that platform.

Your store should implement the state store API. If it's intended to be used as an actor state store, it needs to implement the transactional store API as well. The following sections describe the expected behaviors of these methods.

Init method

The Init method parses the state store metadata and establishes a connection to the underlying store. You can cache the connection or the connected client as a private variable of your store implementation because Dapr creates a singleton instance for each of the registered state stores. This means all requests to a specific state store are handled by the same state store instance. If the underlying state store uses connection pools, you probably don't need to cache the connection, but instead should establish a new connection upon each request. The underlying data store will reuse a connection from its connection pool to carry out the requested operation.

Get method

The Get method returns the value associated with the requested key. It's supposed to return a GetResponse structure with a Data attribute that contains the requested data, and an ETag attribute that holds the corresponding ETag.

If the key is not found, you should return an empty GetResponse instance. You should return any unexpected errors back to the Dapr runtime.

Set method

The Set method inserts or updates the value associated with the requested key. The method is supposed to maintain the corresponding ETag in the same update transaction. Your method should use the SetWithRetries method from *retry.go* (*https:// oreil.ly/rAjdv*) to reuse the Dapr retry library to handle transient errors.

Your code should skip the ETag check if the concurrency option is set to state.Last Write. Otherwise, the code should reject the request if the ETag attached to the request is different from the current ETag in the database.

Delete method

The Delete method removes a key from the underlying state store. Your code should perform similar ETag checks as in the Set method, and it should use the DeleteWi thRetries method that honors the attached retry policy.

BulkDelete and BulkSet methods

The BulkDelete and BulkSet methods carry out Delete and Set operations in batches. However, it's not required to carry out these operations in an isolated transaction. The following sample code is from the default Redis store implementation:

```
func (r *StateStore) BulkDelete(req []state.DeleteRequest) error {
  for _, re := range req {
    err := r.Delete(&re)
    if err != nil {
      return err
    }
  }
  return nil
}
```

Multi method

To implement a transactional store, you need to implement one additional method, Multi, that takes multiple Set and/or Delete operations and handles them as a single transaction. The following code snippet is from the Redis store implementation. As you can see, the method collects requests into an array and uses the Redis client's SendTransaction method to send all the requests as one transaction:

```
func (r *StateStore) Multi(operations []state.TransactionalRequest) error {
  redisReqs := []redis.Request{}
  for _, o := range operations {
    if o.Operation == state.Upsert {
      req := o.Request.(state.SetRequest)
      b, _ := r.json.Marshal(req.Value)
      redisReqs = append(redisReqs, redis.Req("SET", req.Key, b))
    } else if o.Operation == state.Delete {
      req := o.Request.(state.DeleteRequest)
      redisReqs = append(redisReqs, redis.Req("DEL", req.Key))
    }
  }
  _, err := r.client.SendTransaction(context.Background(), redisReqs)
  return err
}
```

In addition to this method, you should also define a New* method to create a new instance of your state store. This method is used by Dapr's component loader when the Dapr sidecar is initialized. The following code sample is also from the default Redis implementation:

```
func NewRedisStateStore() *StateStore {
  return &StateStore{
    json: jsoniter.ConfigFastest,
  }
}
```

Once you are done with your code, run make test from the *components-contribute* root and make sure things compile before moving on to the next step.

Updating the Component Registry

Before your pull request is accepted, you need to update the component reference in your Dapr project to use your local version. To do this, modify the *go.mod* file under the Dapr repository's root folder and add a `replace` directive to redirect the reference to the *github.com/dapr/components-contrib* package to your local folder. For example:

```
replace github.com/dapr/components-contrib v0.0.0-20191014200624-99461da9580e =>
    ../components-contrib
```

Next, modify the state store component loader at *pkg/components/state/loader.go*.

 You need to modify the corresponding component loaders for other component types when you work on those other component types. For example, to modify the loader for pub/sub, modify the *pkg/components/pubsub/loader.go* file instead.

Modify the `Load` method to add a new `RegisterStateStore` call like the following, which registers a new `foo` store type (note in the manifest file the store type has a `state.` prefix, so the full type name is `state.foo`):

```
RegisterStateStore("foo", func() state.Store {
  return etcd.NewFoo()
})
```

Run `make test` to make sure everything builds and all existing test cases still pass.

When you run `make build` or `make test`, Dapr binaries are generated under the *./dist* folder. You can use these binaries to test locally. An easy way to verify if your custom component is in place is to launch the updated Dapr binaries:

```
dapr run --app-id test echo "test"
```

Observe the first entries in Dapr log, and you'll see Dapr has loaded all discovered components. If your component doesn't show up in the list, or if you observe some exceptions, you need to double check your component code and registration code:

```
== DAPR == time="2019-12-28T13:26:13-08:00" level=info msg="starting Dapr Runtime
-- version edge -- commit v0.3.0-rc.0-24-g5faf977-dirty"
== DAPR == time="2019-12-28T13:26:13-08:00" level=info msg="log level set to:
  info"
== DAPR == time="2019-12-28T13:26:13-08:00" level=info msg="standalone mode
configured"
== DAPR == time="2019-12-28T13:26:13-08:00" level=info msg="dapr id: rust-web"
== DAPR == time="2019-12-28T13:26:13-08:00" level=info msg="loaded component
uppercase (middleware.http.uppercase)"
== DAPR == time="2019-12-28T13:26:13-08:00" level=info msg="loaded component
statestore (state.redis)"
== DAPR == time="2019-12-28T13:26:13-08:00" level=info msg="loaded component
messagebus (pubsub.redis)"
```

To test the new binary on Kubernetes, you'll need to generate a new Dapr Docker image and redeploy Dapr onto your Kubernetes cluster. Fortunately, Dapr provides a few build scripts to facilitate the process:

1. First, build the binaries for Linux:

   ```
   make build-linux
   ```

2. Then build the Docker image:

   ```
   export DAPR_REGISTRY=docker.io/<your Docker account>
   export DAPR_TAG=dev
   make docker-build
   make docker-push
   ```

3. If you have previously deployed Dapr using Helm or the build script, remove it first using Helm:

   ```
   helm delete dapr --purge
   ```

4. Finally, deploy the new Dapr build:

   ```
   make docker-deploy-k8s
   ```

Summary

Dapr offers a simple key/value-based state API for applications to store state. The API hides underlying data store details so that the operational concerns are abstracted away from application developers.

Dapr uses a modular architecture that allows new state stores to be plugged in as Dapr components. It ships with Redis as the default state store, but the community has contributed a growing list of data stores that cover many of the popular open source options and cloud platforms.

Dapr supports different concurrency models and consistency models, and it allows additional metadata to be attached to requests in order to leverage store-specific features. Although the state access code is generally portable, you need to understand the subtle differences among store implementations as well as the limitations of specific stores when deciding which state stores to use. You can further customize state handling with a custom middleware that applies additional data transformations such as encryption/decryption, compression, and normalization.

In the next chapter, we'll shift our focus to integration. We'll discuss how Dapr enables various messaging patterns that you can use to build loosely coupled, message-driven microservices applications, and how you can use these patterns to integrate with legacy systems and other cloud services.

CHAPTER 3

Messaging

In a microservices architecture, services in an application are supposed to be isolated from each other so that they can be developed, hosted, upgraded, and scaled independently. Messaging is an important technique to enable flexible communication patterns among these loosely coupled services. As a distributed runtime, Dapr provides built-in messaging support for developers to design event-driven microservices applications.

Event-Driven Programming

Our world is filled with events—indeed, anything that happens can be considered an event. Collision of stars, eruption of a volcano, turn of a page, blink of an eye; these are all events, with different levels of significance associated with them. Some events, such as a blink, rarely cause any significant reactions. Others, such as natural disasters, most certainly do.

Event-driven programming models how events trigger reactions. It has become the pervasive programming model for GUI programs because it presents a natural way to model human–machine interactions—someone clicks a button, and something happens.

Event-driven programming also works well in systems that comprise loosely coupled components. A component notifies other components that something has happened by raising an event, and the event can be picked up by one or more interested listeners and trigger additional actions.

This chapter and the next introduce how Dapr supports event-driven programming using triggers, bindings, and pub/sub.

Messages Versus Events

Events and messages are both data packets that carry some information. However, they have some subtle differences, especially in the way they are handled.

Events indicate that something has already happened. You can't deny the occurrence of an event, because it happened in the past. For example, the fact that you've received a new marketing brochure via email is an event. You can choose to ignore the event, and maybe the brochure itself as well, but you can't change the fact that it was sent to you. The party who triggered an event doesn't usually care if the event is picked up by any listeners. It sends the event to notify any interested parties; what the recipients (if any) do in response is not its concern.

Messages, on the other hand, are sent from a sender to specific recipients. The message sender in this case has the intention to deliver a piece of data to a known party. And it often expects a response from the recipient as well.

Therefore, we talk about *publishing* an event and *sending* a message.

Now let's turn our attention to the recipient's side. To receive certain types of events, a recipient needs to tune in to corresponding channels, which are often called *topics* in this context. This is like tuning your radio to a particular station to listen to your favorite music. In programming, an *event listener* often blocks on waiting for an event, and it handles the events as they come in. A *message recipient*, on the other hand, doesn't need to actively listen to a channel. It can check for messages once in a while and handle received messages one by one or in batches. Of course, a message receiver can also choose to block on waiting for new messages, but it doesn't need to listen on a topic because the messages will be directly delivered to its receiving endpoint.

Messages can be either *pushed* or *pulled*. When a sender knows the addresses of the recipients, it can push the message to all designated recipients. Conversely, recipients who know the sender's address can proactively poll the sender to pull messages down. A single message is normally handled by a single recipient, because once the message is retrieved by one recipient, it's not available to other recipients. This is different from events, which are often broadcast and handled by multiple event handlers.

When a message goes through a series of senders and receivers, it's said to be going through a *pipeline* or a *workflow*. This is also sometimes referred to as *reactive programming*.

For the rest of the chapter, we won't strictly distinguish between the two terms, as the mechanism for passing messages and events is the same. However, it's helpful to maintain a clear understanding of the differences between them.

Input Bindings and Output Bindings

A web service is a recipient of messages or events. Receiving messages is simple—the service simply listens to its endpoint and waits for new messages to arrive. Getting events, however, is trickier. Events are often published through different messaging backbones, which use different authentication and authorization methods, different communication protocols, different APIs, and different delivery approaches (such as push versus pull).

This is where input bindings and output bindings come in. An *input binding* attaches a service to an event source so that the service can be triggered by events from the source. With the binding, a web service can react to messages and external events using the same handler, because the binding gets the event and delivers the event as a message directly to the service's endpoint. An *output binding* allows a service to push messages to a destination. A service can also get responses back from an output binding. In other words, input bindings are one-way communication channels from external systems to your application, and output bindings are two-way communication channels between your application and the external systems.

A binding definition abstracts away all details of the external system. A web service can be attached to any event sources and any event destinations (or "sinks") without any modifications. This is a powerful mechanism that allows the system to be dynamically adapted to different message streams at runtime.

I (Haishi) am quite fond of annoying Yaron by saying things he doesn't like, such as "*Star Trek* is better than *Star Wars*" and "Go is not a real programming language because it doesn't have inheritance and generics." Jokes aside, I sincerely hope Go does support generics one day. If you think about it, the binding mechanism works somewhat like generics—it allows you to design a generic processing pipeline, and then to attach the pipeline to different event streams through bindings.

Bindings allow multiple systems to be "glued" together through the defined pipeline. And connecting to different systems may generate totally different results. For example, Figure 3-1 shows a simple image processing pipeline with three connection points. Binding these points to different services generates different scenarios:

- A typical web service:
    1. Binds to an HTTP input binding
    2. Connects to an AI model (such as GPT-3) that generates summary text
    3. Connects to outbound HTTP to return the results
- A face detection pipeline:
    1. Binds to an event hub that transmits images captured by a camera
    2. Connects to an AI model (such as YOLO) that detects faces

3. Connects to a database to preserve the results

- A smart contract pipeline:

1. Binds to an event hub that transmits scanned documents

2. Connects to an optical character recognition (OCR) service to detect text

3. Sends the detected text to a smart contract to archive the recognized document contents

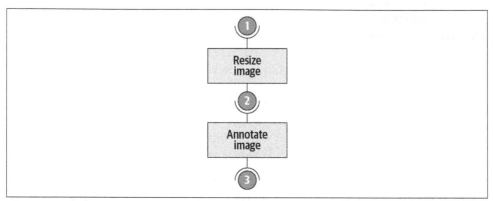

Figure 3-1. Image processing pipeline with bindings

Pub/Sub

We briefly talked about pub/sub back in Chapter 1. As you've seen, Dapr isn't a messaging bus in itself. Instead, Dapr integrates with popular message buses (thanks for our great community contributions!) to deliver messages.

Dapr has chosen to use CloudEvents v1.0 (*https://oreil.ly/FKFGe*) (a CNCF project) as the common event envelope format to improve interoperability across connected services. CloudEvents defines an *event* as representing context and data about an *occurrence*. Events can be delivered through industry standards such as HTTP, AMQP, MQTT, and SMTP. The following is an example (serialized as a JSON document) from the CloudEvents repository:

```
{
    "specversion" : "1.0",
    "type" : "com.github.pull.create",
    "source" : "https://github.com/cloudevents/spec/pull",
    "subject" : "123",
    "id" : "A234-1234-1234",
    "time" : "2018-04-05T17:31:00Z",
    "comexampleextension1" : "value",
    "comexampleothervalue" : 5,
    "datacontenttype" : "text/xml",
    "data" : "<much wow=\"xml\"/>"
}
```

Dapr uses Redis Streams as the default pub/sub messaging backbone. A Redis Stream is an append-only data structure. What's interesting about it is that it allows multiple consumers to block and wait on new data. These consumers are joined to different *consumer groups*, which allows portions of the same stream of messages to be consumed by different consumers without them interfering with each other.

To publish an event to a stream, you use the XADD command with a list of key/value pairs:

```
XADD somestream * device-id 123 reading 35235.6
```

To listen for new items on a stream, you use the XREAD command with the special BLOCK option with a timeout of 0 milliseconds, which means blocking until new data arrives:

```
XREAD BLOCK 0 STREAMS somestream $
```

Note that once a message is read, it's considered to be in a pending state but will not be removed from the stream. The consumer needs to issue the XACK command to permanently remove the message. This kind of extra acknowledgment is commonly required by messaging systems to ensure a message is processed at least once. Essentially, the consumer uses XACK to signify the successful processing of a message. If a consumer crashes before it can send the XACK command, it can pick up the same message the next time, when it recovers.

Redis also provides an XCLAIM command to reclaim pending messages from a permanently failed consumer. We won't discuss that command further in this context.

That's about as much as theoretical stuff as we'll cover. Now it's time to put pub/sub into action!

Pub/Sub with Dapr

In this walk-through, we'll use PowerShell to write a script that subscribes to a topic and prints out the received messages on the console.

Implementing the PowerShell Script

The PowerShell script needs to do two things. First, it needs to listen to a /dapr/ subscribe route and return the names of any topics to subscribe to (A, in the following example) as a JSON array upon request. Second, it needs to listen to the relevant routes (here, /A), waiting for Dapr to post events.

Create a new *app.ps1* file with the following contents:

```
$httpServer = [System.Net.HttpListener]::new()
$httpServer.Prefixes.Add("http://localhost:3000/")
$httpServer.Start()
```

```
while ($httpServer.IsListening) {
    $context = $httpServer.GetContext()
    if ($context.Request.HttpMethod -eq 'GET' -and $context.Request.RawUrl
      -eq '/dapr/subscribe') {
        $buffer = [System.Text.Encoding]::UTF8.GetBytes("[{topic: 'A',
          route: '/A']")
        $context.Response.ContentLength64 = $buffer.Length
        $context.Response.ContentType = "application/json"
        $context.Response.OutputStream.Write($buffer, 0, $buffer.Length)
        $context.Response.OutputStream.Close()
    }
    if ($context.Request.HttpMethod -eq 'POST' -and $context.Request.RawUrl
      -eq '/A') {
        $length = $context.Request.ContentLength64
        $buffer = [System.Byte[]]::CreateInstance([System.Byte],$length)
        $context.Request.InputStream.Read($buffer,0,$length)
        $message = [System.Text.Encoding]::UTF8.GetString($buffer)
        write-host $message
        $buffer = [System.Text.Encoding]::UTF8.GetBytes("OK")
        $context.Response.ContentLength64 = $buffer.Length
        $context.Response.OutputStream.Write($buffer, 0, $buffer.Length)
        $context.Response.OutputStream.Close()
    }
}
```

The script is quite straightforward—it launches an HTTP listener and listens to the aforementioned route. When it receives a GET request to the /dapr/subscribe route,[1] it returns a JSON array with a subscription to topic A at route /A. When it receives a POST request to the /A route, it prints out the received message.

Testing Pub/Sub with the Dapr CLI

The Dapr CLI has a built-in command that can be used to publish messages to a topic. This is very convenient for testing pub/sub. We'll use the command in this exercise:

1. Make sure you have Redis running locally. If not, you can launch a new Redis server using Docker:

   ```
   docker run --name redis -d redis
   ```

2. Launch the PowerShell script using Dapr:

   ```
   dapr run --app-id ps --port 3500 --app-port 3000 --protocol http cmd /c
     "powershell -f app.ps1"
   ```

---

1 At the time of writing, supporting multiple pub/sub components is being added. See the online documentation for possible route/payload format changes.

---

3. Use the Dapr CLI to send a test message:

    ```
    dapr publish --topic A --payload "{ \"message\": \"This is a test\" }"
    ```

4. You should see the message displayed in the PowerShell console.

 For interested readers, Dapr's sample repository (*https://oreil.ly/ pjPg_*) includes an extensive example that involves two subscribers and a GUI publisher.

Dapr Pub/Sub Behaviors

As mentioned earlier, Dapr ensures at-least-once message delivery. If your application needs to process a message *exactly* once, you'll need to implement your own tracking method—such as using a state store—to make sure you don't handle the same transaction multiple times. Regardless, your application might get triggered with the same message and you'll have to handle deduplication in your application logic.

A message is published to all subscribers. However, if you have multiple Dapr instances with the same application ID, only one of the instances will get the message. This is useful when you use the *competing consumer* pattern to drain a topic with multiple instances. Because each of the messages will be sent to only one of the instances, the instances can collectively handle pending messages by sharing the workload.

Extending Dapr Pub/Sub

Dapr pub/sub components work in a similar fashion to other Dapr component types, such as state store components. At the time of writing, the Dapr community has contributed a few pub/sub components, including for Redis Streams, NATS, Azure Service Bus, and RabbitMQ.

Dapr defines a simple interface for pub/sub, as shown in the following code snippet:

```
type PubSub interface {
    Init(metadata Metadata) error
    Publish(req *PublishRequest) error
    Subscribe(req SubscribeRequest, handler func(msg *NewMessage) error) error
}
```

You should initialize the connection to the messaging backbone in the `Init` method. You are also expected to automatically provision the topic in the `Publish` method and the `Subscribe` method. The following code snippet shows the default Redis implementation:

```
func (r *redisStreams) Publish(req *pubsub.PublishRequest) error {
    _, err := r.client.XAdd(&redis.XAddArgs{
```

```
        Stream: req.Topic,
        Values: map[string]interface{}{"data": req.Data},
    }).Result()
    if err != nil {
        return fmt.Errorf("redis streams: error from publish: %s", err)
    }

    return nil
}

func (r *redisStreams) Subscribe(req pubsub.SubscribeRequest,
    handler func(msg *pubsub.NewMessage) error) error {
    err := r.client.XGroupCreateMkStream(req.Topic,
      r.metadata.consumerID, "0").Err()
    if err != nil {
        log.Warnf("redis streams: %s", err)
    }
    go r.beginReadingFromStream(req.Topic, r.metadata.consumerID, handler)
    return nil
}
```

At the time of writing, Dapr doesn't support dynamic topic subscription. Because this is a frequently requested feature, it's likely to be implemented soon (and may have been by the time you're reading this text). Until then, however, your application needs to configure its own routes on start to subscribe to selected topics and then listen to the corresponding routes.

Input and Output Bindings with Dapr

Input and output bindings are component types in Dapr. Input bindings monitor event sources and trigger application logic when new messages are received. Output bindings write messages to external message sinks. To use an input binding, you need to define a manifest file that describes the binding. Then, to get messages from a bound topic, you listen to a path with the same name as the topic for POST requests. To send a message to an output binding, make a POST request to the /v1.0/bind ings/<topic name> endpoint on the Dapr sidecar.

At the time of writing, Dapr supports several input and output bindings, as summarized in Table 3-1.

Table 3-1. Dapr input and output bindings

Name	Input binding	Output binding
HTTP		Yes
Kafka	Yes	Yes
Kubernetes events	Yes	
MQTT	Yes	Yes
RabbitMQ	Yes	Yes

Name	Input binding	Output binding
Redis		Yes
Twilio SMS		Yes
AWS DynamoDB		Yes
AWS S3		Yes
AWS SNS		Yes
AWS SQS	Yes	Yes
Azure Blob storage		Yes
Azure Cosmos DB		Yes
Azure Event Hubs	Yes	Yes
Azure Service Bus queues	Yes	Yes
Azure SignalR		Yes
GCP Cloud Pub/Sub	Yes	Yes
Google Cloud Storage buckets		Yes

Using Input Bindings

The following YAML file is a sample input binding manifest that describes a Kafka input binding that is bound to a `topic1` topic:

```
apiVersion: dapr.io/v1alpha1
kind: Component
metadata:
  name: myEvent
spec:
  type: bindings.kafka
  metadata:
  - name: topics
    value: topic1
  - name: brokers
    value: localhost:9092
  - name: consumerGroup
    value: group1
```

When new messages are received, Dapr posts the messages to the corresponding end-point hosted by your application through POST calls. For example, to subscribe to a `sample-topic` trigger, your code needs to listen to a `/sample-topic` route, as shown in the following Node.js code snippet:

```
app.post('/sample-topic', (req, res) => {
    console.log(req.body);
    res.status(200).send();
});
```

To inform Dapr that your application has successfully processed a message, you need to return a 200 status code when you finish processing the message. Otherwise, Dapr assumes that processing failed and will attempt to redeliver the message. Although

Dapr has some retry logic, message delivery is not automatically ensured.[2] Instead, it's up to the input binding implementation to choose how messages are delivered, such as *at least once* or *best attempt*.

Using Output Bindings

In order to send a message to an output binding, you send the message payload encoded in the `data` field of a JSON document to the endpoint `/v1.0/bindings/` *<topic name>*, as shown in the following Python code from Dapr's sample repository (*https://oreil.ly/mtinI*):

```
import time
import requests
import os

dapr_port = os.getenv("DAPR_HTTP_PORT", 3500)

dapr_url = "http://localhost:{}/v1.0/bindings/sample-topic".format(dapr_port)
n = 0
while True:
    n += 1
    payload = { "data": {"orderId": n}}
    print(payload, flush=True)
    try:
        response = requests.post(dapr_url, json=payload)
        print(response.text, flush=True)

    except Exception as e:
        print(e)

    time.sleep(1)
```

Implementing Input Bindings

Input bindings are defined by an `InputBinding` interface:

```
type InputBinding interface {
    Init(metadata Metadata) error
    Read(handler func(*ReadResponse) error) error
}
```

The `read` method is supposed to be a blocking method—it should block and never return throughout its life span. It waits for messages from the message source and calls the specified callback function (usually in a separate Go routine) when new messages arrive. The following code snippet shows the Kafka trigger implementation. You

---

2 Dapr team is working on providing automatic retries across all Dapr components, include bindings.

can see how the read method keeps looping to consume events from the topic until the process is forcibly terminated by system break signals:

```go
func (k *Kafka) Read(handler func(*bindings.ReadResponse) error) error {
    config := sarama.NewConfig()
    config.Version = sarama.V1_0_0_0
    if k.authRequired {
        updateAuthInfo(config, k.saslUsername, k.saslPassword)
    }
    c := consumer {
        callback: handler,
        ready:    make(chan bool),
    }

    client, err := sarama.NewConsumerGroup(k.brokers, k.consumerGroup, config)
    if err != nil {
        return err
    }

    ctx, cancel := context.WithCancel(context.Background())

    wg := &sync.WaitGroup{}
    wg.Add(1)
    go func() {
        defer wg.Done()
        for {
            if err = client.Consume(ctx, k.topics, &c); err != nil {
                log.Errorf("error from c: %s", err)
            }
            // check if context was cancelled, signaling that the c should stop
            if ctx.Err() != nil {
                return
            }
            c.ready = make(chan bool)
        }
    }()

    <-c.ready

    sigterm := make(chan os.Signal, 1)
    signal.Notify(sigterm, syscall.SIGINT, syscall.SIGTERM)
    <-sigterm
    cancel()
    wg.Wait()
    if err = client.Close(); err != nil {
        return err
    }
    return nil
}
```

Implementing Output Bindings

The output binding interface is just as simple:

```
type OutputBinding interface {
    Init(metadata Metadata) error
    Invoke(req *InvokeRequest) (InvokeResponse, error)
    Operations() []OperationKind
}
```

To implement an output binding, you initialize a connection to the downstream event target in the `Init` method and write the given event to the destination using the `Invoke` method. If the `Invoke` method returns without any errors, the message is considered to have been sent successfully.

Implementing an output binding is quite straightforward. One afternoon, Mark Russinovich decided to give it a try. Although he wasn't very familiar with the Go language at the time, he was able to implement a functional Twilio SMS output binding in just a couple of hours. The implementation uses Twilio's HTTP REST API to send SMS messages to the designated recipient configured in the output binding metadata:

```
func (t *SMS) Invoke(req *bindings.InvokeRequest) (*bindings.InvokeResponse,
        error) {
    toNumberValue := t.metadata.toNumber
    if toNumberValue == "" {
        toNumberFromRequest, ok := req.Metadata[toNumber]
        if !ok || toNumberFromRequest == "" {
            return nil, errors.New("twilio missing \"toNumber\" field")
        }
        toNumberValue = toNumberFromRequest
    }

    v := url.Values{}
    v.Set("To", toNumberValue)
    v.Set("From", t.metadata.fromNumber)
    v.Set("Body", string(req.Data))
    vDr := *strings.NewReader(v.Encode())

    twilioURL := fmt.Sprintf("%s%s/Messages.json", twilioURLBase,
        t.metadata.accountSid)
    httpReq, err := http.NewRequest("POST", twilioURL, &vDr)
    if err != nil {
        return nil, err
    }
    httpReq.SetBasicAuth(t.metadata.accountSid, t.metadata.authToken)
    httpReq.Header.Add("Accept", "application/json")
    httpReq.Header.Add("Content-Type", "application/x-www-form-urlencoded")

    resp, err := t.httpClient.Do(httpReq)
    if err != nil {
        return nil, err
```

```
    }
    defer resp.Body.Close()
    if !(resp.StatusCode >= 200 && resp.StatusCode < 300) {
        return nil, fmt.Errorf("error from Twilio: %s", resp.Status)
    }
    return nil, nil
}
```

The `Invoke` method can return results from the connected systems through the `bind ings.InvokeResponse` return parameter. This allows applications to get responses from external systems while dispatching messages to those systems.

An output binding can also define types of operations it supports through the `Opera tions` method. For example, the following code snippet defines that an output binding supports the `Create` operation:

```
func (c *CosmosDB) Operations() []bindings.OperationKind {
    return []bindings.OperationKind{bindings.CreateOperation}
}
```

Autoscaling with KEDA

Kubernetes-based Event Driven Autoscaling (KEDA) is another project initiated by Yaron to autoscale pods based on the queue length of a messaging backbone such as Azure Event Hubs, Kafka, NATS, or RabbitMQ.

What makes KEDA extra-interesting is its capability of scaling from/to zero. When there are no events coming in, KEDA can remove all app pods so that the hosting cost of your application while idle is reduced to a minimum. When new events come in, KEDA temporarily holds the events as it spins up a pod and then dispatches the held events to the pod. Then it serves as a Kubernetes metrics server that feeds metrics to the Kubernetes Horizontal Pod Autoscaler for further scaling.

You control KEDA's behavior through a `ScaleObject` custom resource. The following is a sample `ScaleObject` that scales the `message-processor` deployment when an item appears on the `myQueueItem` Azure Storage queue:

```
apiVersion: keda.k8s.io/v1alpha1
kind: ScaledObject
metadata:
  name: message-processor
  namespace: default
  labels:
    deploymentName: message-processor
spec:
  scaleTargetRef:
    deploymentName: message-processor
  triggers:
  - type: azure-queue
    metadata:
```

```
name: myQueueItem
type: queueTrigger
queueName: items
queueLength: "1"
connection: AzureWebJobsStorage
```

You can use KEDA to implement patterns such as competing consumer. Figure 3-2 illustrates a message-driven system that uses bindings to exchange data between a producer and a consumer. The consumer in this case is automatically scaled by KEDA. When the producer is not generating any events, all consumers are terminated. As the queue length increases, more and more consumers are spun up to drain the request queue quickly. Dapr sends only one copy of each message to one of the consumer instances sharing the same application ID. In other words, the consumer instances are competing to get the messages processed—hence the "competing consumer" pattern name.

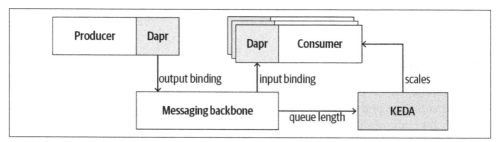

Figure 3-2. Competing consumer pattern with KEDA autoscaling

You can also use KEDA to scale an entire processing pipeline to zero when there are no events to be processed, as shown in Figure 3-3. This suits systems that are occasionally triggered, or systems that have seasonal or periodic traffic. All you pay for is a monitoring pod (assuming you are using an ideal serverless hosting environment that charges by pod minutes) when the system is idle.

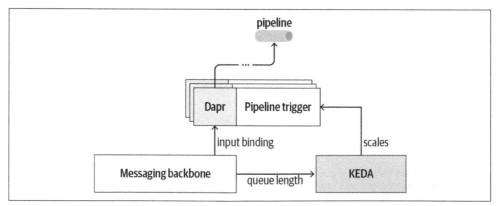

Figure 3-3. Using KEDA to scale an entire pipeline

Next, we'll go through a few messaging patterns and explain how they could be implemented using Dapr. There are many messaging patterns out there, and our choices are somewhat arbitrary. We hope the selection represents a set of distinct messaging scenarios, but it's by no means a comprehensive list.

Messaging Patterns

Message-based systems are like LEGO sets: you can assemble smaller pieces into interesting patterns. This section covers a select few patterns that you can compose using Dapr's triggers and connectors.

The Saga Pattern

Many complex workflows involve calling distributed services from different service providers. For example, to book a trip, you'll need to carry out several distributed transactions, including booking a flight, booking a hotel, and booking a rental car. If any of the transactions fails, you may want to retry the failed transaction, or you may want to roll back all the transactions. Calling several services is not difficult. Handling different failing conditions is tricky. This section discusses how you can implement distributed transactions with the Saga pattern using Dapr connectors.

The original idea of the Saga pattern is to break a long-lived transaction (LLT) into a sequence of smaller transactions to avoid long holds on database records. The pattern works well in distributed systems where such long holds (or universal locks) are impossible.

The transactions in the Saga pattern can be coordinated by a central coordinator, or by event triggers. In the case of a central coordinator, the coordinator calls each service and tracks the state of the overall transaction. In the case of event triggers, when a transaction finishes, it triggers the next transaction by sending an event.

Using a central coordinator

Figure 3-4 illustrates how a central coordinator coordinates distributed transactions. The coordinator calls individual services in turn to complete the overall workflow, and it saves its state to a persistent state store so that it can recover from crashes. One way to write the coordinator is to use Dapr actors with a Dapr state store. When you use Dapr actors, each distributed transaction is identified by a unique actor ID. This allows multiple distributed transactions to execute in parallel. To make a transaction self-driven, you can use an actor reminder or timer to have it periodically check its own state and take the necessary actions to drive the transaction to completion.

If any of the steps fails, the coordinator will invoke the corresponding service provider to cancel the transaction. You can also apply flexible policies in transaction handling, such as finding alternatives when a certain booking can't be made. Of course, this means writing more code, but you get a finer grade of control in return.

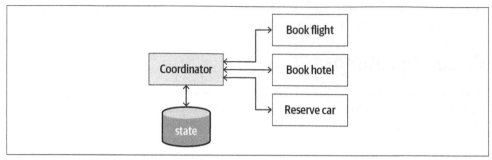

Figure 3-4. Distributed transactions with a central coordinator

Using events

Another way to implement the Saga pattern is to use events to trigger the next steps as the workflow progresses.Figure 3-5 shows a design that triggers transactional steps through a series of events. The workflow is initiated by an external event, such as a submission from a web interface. Then the first transaction is executed. Upon completion, the first transaction raises an event to trigger the second transaction, and so on.

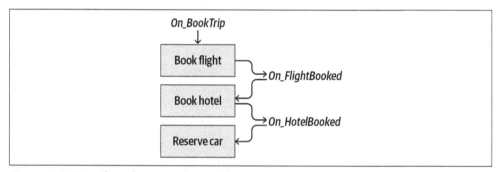

Figure 3-5. Distributed transactions with events

This strategy usually works well for a simple workflow with a few transactions. The design allows maximum parallelization, and it allows different service providers to be swapped out without affecting the overall workflow. For example, the *Book Hotel* transaction handler can be replaced by a more advanced handler that subscribes to the same event but tries several hotels to make a reservation.

You can also change the overall topology of the handling system on the fly. For example, you can have multiple transaction handlers subscribing to the same On_BookTrip event and attempt to perform multiple bookings in parallel.

When the workflow becomes more complex, however, tracking what's happening becomes difficult. Testing is also harder because of the distributed nature of the system. Figure 3-6 shows a more comprehensive view of the messaging system when failures are considered. When any of the transaction handlers fails to make a reservation, it raises a separate event (such as On_CarOutOfStock) to negate the transaction. Eventually, a billing service responds at the end of the event chain and refunds the user. As you can see, the number of events and the complexity of interactions among transaction handlers increases rapidly when you consider different possibilities.

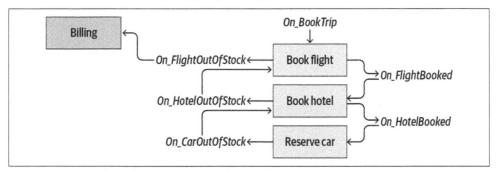

Figure 3-6. Distributed transactions with cancelation events

The workflow may also come to a halt if some of the messages are lost. And because of the at-least-once delivery behavior, you will have to make sure you don't double-book.

In summary, making a highly parallel, highly reliable workflow system with distributed transactions takes quite some work. At the time of writing, the Dapr team is actively working on the workflow feature that uses a Dapr actor as the stateful coordinator (Dapr workflow). We'll also work with existing products and open source projects to improve interoperability across different workflow systems. This may require adoption of a common workflow description language, or a series of translation layers that can translate among description formats.

Regardless, Dapr's workflow engine aims to be self-contained, lightweight, and highly parallelized. For example, after we build up the dependency tree of the workflow actions, we'll try to execute actions in parallel when possible, and we'll allow the "any of the *n* actions" pattern, in which an action can wait and resume when any of the upstream actions completes.

Content-Based Routing

Listening to an event source comes with a certain cost. At minimum, you need to maintain a connection to the event source in order to pick up new events. When you have many different types of message handlers interested in the same event source, keeping many concurrent connections to the same event source open can be inefficient or impractical. In such cases, you may want to set up a central message dispatcher that subscribes to the event source and dispatches messages to different handlers based on message headers or message bodies. Figure 3-7 shows a message dispatcher sending messages to different handlers based on message contents.

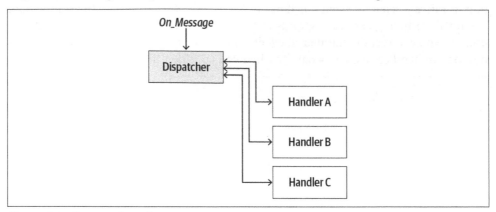

Figure 3-7. Content-based routing

Content-based routing is useful when you have multiple message handler candidates to process a single message. Remember that each of the handlers may have been designed without any integrations in mind. A handler may simply fail when it sees an unrecognized message format. If they all subscribe to the original On_Message event and act on their own, it will be hard to track if a message is processed multiple times, or whether it is processed at all. When you use the content-based routing pattern, the dispatcher examines the incoming messages and dispatches them to the most appropriate handler.

The dispatcher is stateless, because examining a single message has nothing to do with other messages. You can scale out the dispatcher (by using the competing consumer pattern, for example) to avoid it becoming a bottleneck.

You can also extend the pattern with a *dead letter queue*. When a dispatcher detects a message that can't be processed by any of the handlers, it can enqueue the message to a dead letter queue, which will be examined and cleansed by an offline process.

Routing Slip

In a complex message-based system, message handlers are interconnected by the messaging backbone to form convoluted message pipelines with many different paths. If you want to control the exact path a message picks, you can attach a *routing slip* to the message. The routing slip defines the path the message is supposed to go through. When a handler completes its operation, it checks itself off on the routing slip and sends the message to the next recipient on the list. The entries on the routing slip can be handler addresses, but that will tightly couple the handlers together. Instead, these entries can be message topics through which the handlers are connected, as shown in Figure 3-8.

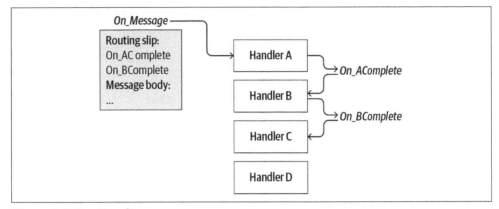

Figure 3-8. Routing slip

The main benefit of the routing slip pattern is the ability to dynamically configure message routes per message. The pattern allows distributed, asynchronous, parallel message processing while ensuring a predefined flow is precisely carried out without a central message coordinator.

Smart Proxy

As described earlier, Dapr uses a sidecar architecture to deliver common functionalities such as state management and messaging to applications. What if we extend Dapr and allow it to deliver arbitrary functionalities, such as face detection, to an application? In other words, what if an application can dynamically acquire and consume any required functionalities through Dapr?

This is indeed a fascinating idea. However, a lot of work would be needed to make it a reality. How does an application describe its intention? How is the intention translated into search criteria for matching capabilities? How is the capability consumed? All these questions must be answered. We believe a new architectural paradigm, which we call Capability Oriented Architecture (COA), is needed to systematically address these issues. A detailed discussion of COA is out of the scope of this book. Instead, we'll discuss a simpler but also useful pattern: the smart proxy pattern.

A smart proxy exposes a local endpoint for a client to call and then uses a combination of various technologies to bring in the required capabilities. For example, it may directly call a remote service, or it may send a message to a downstream handler and wait for a response. It may even invoke a complex workflow that downloads a Docker image, launches it, and then makes a call to an endpoint exposed by the Docker container. Regardless of what's happening behind the proxy, the client calling the proxy sees only a simple, direct service invocation through the local host.

Figure 3-9 shows a possible configuration of a Dapr sidecar acting as a smart proxy. You can see the proxy uses different technologies to invoke required services and return the results to the caller in the context of a single service call.

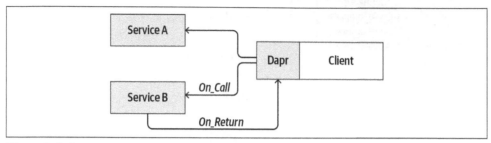

Figure 3-9. Smart proxy

The smart proxy pattern really shines in edge computing scenarios. Many low-power devices need to deliver required functionalities to end users in context. However, they are often constrained by on-chip capability and power consumption. By using a smart proxy, they can delegate service calls to field gateways, LAN-based servers, or cloud services and return the call results to the caller.

MapReduce

The MapReduce pattern splits a big task into smaller tasks and runs the small tasks in parallel. Then the results from the smaller tasks are aggregated into the final output of the original task.

There are several different ways to implement the MapReduce pattern using Dapr. For example, you can use the competing consumer pattern with a Dapr actor. When the actor receives the big task, it can split the task up into smaller tasks and enqueue these small tasks to a queue. Then task processors that subscribe to the queue can compete to finish all the tasks. When a processor completes a small task, it calls back to the actor to report the result. Each time the actor receives a callback, it increments an internal counter. When the counter matches with the number of generated tasks, the actor aggregates the results and generates the final output, as shown in Figure 3-10.

> The turn-based concurrency ensures concurrent calls to the actor are sequentialized, so there won't be conflicts in incrementing the counters. See Chapter 5 for more on actors.

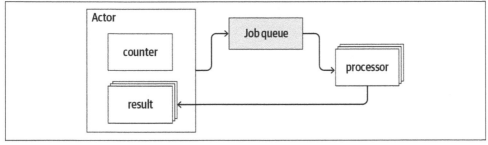

Figure 3-10. MapReduce pattern

When the data volume is huge, you can opt to save data to an external storage and send only data indexes to task processors. Similarly, the data processor can write the result back to an external database. When all the tasks complete, the actor can assemble the result from the database.

This concludes our discussion of messaging patterns. Again, we've only picked a handful out of tens of useful messaging patterns; for readers who are interested in learning more, we recommend *Enterprise Integration Patterns* by Gregor Hohpe and Bobby Woolf (Addison-Wesley Professional).

Summary

Messaging is a very powerful tool for designing loosely coupled microservices systems. Dapr provides common messaging constructs such as pub/sub and bindings, but it doesn't create its own messaging backbone. Instead, it integrates with popular messaging backbones to deliver these capabilities.

Dapr pub/sub allows message publishers to publish messages to a topic, and all subscribers of the topic to get copies of the messages. Dapr ensures a message is processed at least once.

Dapr input bindings can be used to trigger applications by events from any of the supported event sources. Dapr output bindings allow applications to connect to popular external systems to exchange data. Bindings allow you to define a generic processing pipeline that can be dynamically attached to different external systems.

In the next chapter, we'll cover another fundamental topic: security.

CHAPTER 4

Security

The internet is a hostile environment. Security is not an option but a necessity. When you design your application, security has to be an integral part of the design, not something you add on at a later phase. When it comes to security, the goal of Dapr is to make applications *secure by default*. That means you should get common security best practices out of the box by default, and you can then fine-tune the system to satisfy your security requirements. Dapr is still a young project and our journey toward this goal is far from finished, but this chapter introduces how we design Dapr components so that we can plug in security features and bring best practices to your applications in the most natural way.

Securing a Distributed Application

To secure a system you need to consider several challenges, including access control, data protection, secured communication, intrusion and abnormality detection, and user privacy. Dapr's long-term goal is to help you to address these challenges as much as possible so that your applications will be secure by default.

Because Dapr is still in its infancy, we still have a long way to go. This chapter begins by discussing some of our thoughts on security, to give you an idea of the general directions Dapr security is taking. Then the chapter will cover what we've implemented in Dapr. Chances are that by the time you read this text, Dapr will have put more security features at your disposal. And of course, if you have any feedback or suggestions, please submit issues to the Dapr repository (*https://oreil.ly/mF5LO*).

Let's start with the most obvious area of concern: access control.

Access Control

Securing a central server is relatively easy, as you have full control of the hosting environment. For example, you can set up firewall rules and load balancer policies to limit accesses to specific client IP segments and ports. You also can integrate with central identity providers such as Active Directory to enable centralized authentication and authorization.

 These two terms are often confused. Simply put, authentication answers the question "Who are you?" and authorization answers the question "What are you allowed to do?"

When you host your application in the cloud, you should leverage the security features the cloud platform provides. Modern cloud platforms offer security features that are similar to what you have available on premises, so you can manage access control using familiar technologies and concepts such as network security groups, RBAC, certificate-based authentication, and firewalls.

Things become more complicated when you're trying to manage the security of a distributed system, because you often need to deal with scattered compute resources, untrusted connections, and heterogeneous technology stacks. You'll have to rethink your strategies when dealing with common security challenges such as establishing identity, setting access control policies, and communicating over the network.

Identity

An application needs to deal with two types of identity: user identity and service identity. A user identity identifies a specific user, while a service identity represents a service or a process. You can define access control policies (discussed next) for both types of identity. For example, you can grant a user identity read access to a relational database table, and you can constrain a service identity from making any outbound connections.

Services like Microsoft Azure Active Directory (AAD) allow you to establish and manage identities for both users and services. In such cases, AAD is referred as a *trusted identity provider* (IP), and your application is a *relying party* (RP) of the IP. The IP issues *security tokens* to trusted RPs. RPs extract *claims* from the tokens and make authorization decisions based on the claims. For instance, when you go to rent a car, the car rental company (the RP) requires a security token, which is your driver's license in this case, issued by a trusted IP—the Department of Motor Vehicles (DMV). A claim is a statement made about a particular property of that token. In the case of a driver's license, the name on the license is a claim made by the DMV about the name property of the holder. Because the RP trusts the IP and the issued security token, the RP takes every claim made by the token—name, address, age, eye color, etc.—to be true. This design of delegating authentication to a trusted IP is called a *claim-based architecture.*

From Dapr's perspective, establishing the user's identity is an application concern. Dapr can build up utilities, such as the OAuth middleware you saw in Chapter 1, to facilitate authentication and authorization processes under popular protocols such as OAuth 2.0, WS-Federation, and decentralized identifiers (DIDs). But Dapr will not be opinionated about how your applications choose to identify users and impose access control policies.

Dapr has the potential to provide great assistance in establishing service identity. As you saw in theIntroduction, each Dapr instance is identified by a unique string name. If we can harden the name, we can use the Dapr ID as the service identity of the application that the Dapr sidecar represents. For example, one possibility is for Dapr to integrate with AAD Pod Identity, which allows Kubernetes applications to access cloud resources and services securely with AAD.

Access control policies

Because Dapr sidecars sit on service invocation paths, Dapr can provide more assistance with fine-grained access control. For example, Dapr can apply an access policy to a /foo route to allow access only from explicitly allowed Dapr IDs through specific HTTP verbs (such as GET). Before this feature is implemented by the Dapr runtime itself, you can author a custom middleware to provide such filtering. The following pseudocode shows how a filter can be defined using Dapr middleware:

```
func (m *Middleware) GetHandler(metadata middleware.Metadata)
    (func(h fasthttp.RequestHandler) fasthttp.RequestHandler, error) {
 ...

    return func(h fasthttp.RequestHandler) fasthttp.RequestHandler {
        return func(ctx *fasthttp.RequestCtx) {
            if (ctx.IsGet() && ctx.Path == "/foo") {
                h(ctx);
            } else {
                // Deny access
            }
        }
    }, nil
}
```

What's even more interesting is that Dapr can reinforce similar access control policies when messaging is used. For example, a Dapr sidecar can reject requests to publish to certain topics or forbid an application to read from certain topics.

Such policies can be captured by middleware configurations or other metadata formats, and reinforcement of the policies is completely separated from the application code. This is exactly the kind of separation of concerns Dapr aims to provide to dis-tributed application developers. Combined with Dapr's tracing feature, such an access control mechanism also provides full visibility into how access is granted or denied.

Network security

Access controls can also be implemented at the network layer. Many microservice systems use *service meshes* to manage the dynamic network environment. Dapr is designed to work well with existing service mesh solutions such as Consul and Istio. Figure 4-1 illustrates how Dapr sidecars can be laid on top of service mesh envoys to provide additional access control and filtering on top of network policies that are reinforced by a service mesh.

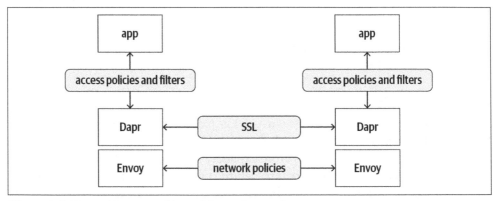

Figure 4-1. Dapr sidecar working with service mesh envoy

For example, the following Consul service rules, written in HashiCorp Configuration Language (HCL), allow read access to any services without prefixes and write access to the "app" services. The rules also deny all access to the "admin" service. These rules are enforced by Consul, and Dapr (and the app) remains oblivious in this case:

```
service_prefix "" {
  policy = "read"
}
service "app" {
  policy = "write"
}
service "admin" {
  policy = "deny"
}
```

One thing to be aware of is that Dapr provides mutual TLS, a feature that is common in service meshes. Thus, when you configure Dapr to work with a service mesh, you'll probably want to disable one of the TLS layers. Please consult the Dapr documenta-tion (*https://oreil.ly/0ginb*) for instructions and recommendations.

Even when appropriate service access control policies are in place, we still need to go a level deeper and protect the data on which these services operate. We'll look at data protection next.

Data Protection

When it comes to protecting data, there are three areas we need to consider: data at rest, data in transit, and data in use.

Protecting data at rest

A common way to protect data at rest is to use encryption. At the time of writing, Dapr doesn't provide data encryption out of the box, but automatic encryption/decryption features might be added to its state store in the future. Dapr also has a built-in feature to manage secrets, which we'll introduce later in this chapter. You can use this feature to manage encryption keys for user data.

Dapr doesn't concern itself with data backup and restore; this is a responsibility we believe should be taken up by the underlying data store or through specialized backup/restore solutions.

Protecting data in transit

Dapr sidecars use SSL tunnels when communicating with each other, so data is exchanged through secured channels. This avoids threats such as eavesdropping and man-in-the-middle attacks.

When Dapr sends and receives messages to and from a messaging backbone, it authenticates against the corresponding service using that service's required authentication method. Most of these services require secured channels when data is exchanged.

If desired, applications can apply additional data integration protections such as encryption and digital signatures. Those are application concerns and are not covered by Dapr.

You might be wondering whether an encryption/decryption middleware could be developed to provide automatic encryption/decryption before the data is put on the wire. This would work, but with one caveat: Dapr tracing middleware is inserted at the top of the middleware stack. This means data may get logged in plain text (when logging the message body is enabled) before it hits the encryption layer. We think this is a reasonable design, because encrypted logs are harder to use in diagnosis. If you need to scramble some sensitive data before it's logged, you can write a custom exporter to obfuscate certain data fields, such as personally identifiable information (PII), before writing the log to downstream systems.

Finally, the best way to protect data in transit is to not transfer data at all. The Dapr actor model, which we'll introduce in Chapter 5, provides state encapsulation so that an actor's state is maintained only by the actor itself. For instance, instead of sending a procurement order across services, you can encapsulate an order as an actor. All possible actions on the order are conducted through the methods exposed by the actor.

There are established methods and protocols for both protecting data at rest and protecting data in transit. Protecting data in use, which we'll briefly cover next, is much trickier.

Protecting data in use

No matter how data is encrypted and protected at rest and during transit, it is usually processed in plain text. The probability of a hacker gaining access to a running process is low. However, such attacks often aim at high-value targets, such as financial information or access keys. Some of the worst information leaks have been traced back to rogue insiders, who sometimes had administrative access.

The situation is even more complicated on the edge. For example, one unique challenge with edge computing (compared to the cloud) is that an adversary can join a tampered-with device to the compute plane to capture sensitive user information.

Fortunately, there are a few possible ways to protect data from privileged users. For example, *confidential computing* uses a *trusted execution environment* (TEE, a.k.a. *enclave*). A software- or hardware-based TEE creates an isolated execution environment that can't be observed from the outside by anyone, even the system administrator. A TEE can request attestation (a mechanism for software to prove its identity) to ensure only approved code is executed.

At the algorithm level, secure multiparty computation (MPC) allows multiple parties to jointly compute a function over their inputs while keeping the inputs private, and homomorphic encryption allows calculations (such as AI trainings and inferences) be performed on encrypted data.

At the time of writing, Dapr doesn't have a plan to aid in protecting data during use. One possible way for Dapr to help in confidential computing is to integrate with the Open Enclave SDK (*https://oreil.ly/e7Snk*) to encapsulate enclave creation, code deployment, attestation, and communication between trusted components and untrusted components. Dapr can also be extended to support certain MPC scenarios. For example, a custom Dapr middleware may provide homomorphic encryption so that data can be processed while encrypted. Additionally, some machine learning models can be adapted to run inference on encrypted data, and the encrypted results can be decrypted only by the original data owner.

Secured Communication

We touched upon secured communication when we discussed protecting data in transit in the previous section. However, there's another transmission channel we need to consider: the communication channel between a Dapr sidecar and the application process it serves. In a sidecar architecture, the sidecar and the application it attaches to are in the same security domain, in which they can communicate with each other in plain text. However, we've heard from our customers that they want in-depth protection with secured channels between the Dapr sidecar and the application. This makes sense because the Dapr sidecar also works as an independent process. At the time of writing, this feature has been put on the roadmap; please consult the online documentation for updates.

Intrusion and Abnormality Detection

Although Dapr has no intrusion or abnormality detection capabilities out of the box, integrating with such systems is not a far-fetched goal. For example, a custom Dapr middleware can send data packet duplicates to a machine learning–based abnormality detection system for both training and inference purposes, and this can be done transparently without interfering with the application itself.

Dapr does provide proactive rate limiting to avoid excessive numbers of service calls. This is done through a community-contributed middleware. The implementation uses Tollbooth (*https://oreil.ly/40fJO*), a generic middleware for rate-limiting HTTP requests based on the Token Bucket algorithm. The algorithm puts tokens into an imaginary bucket at a fixed rate. Each request consumes a certain number of tokens, proportional to the message size. When a request comes in, if there are enough tokens in the bucket to be "spent" on the request, the request goes through. Otherwise, the request is rejected. When a request is rejected, the response will contain headers such as `X-Rate-Limit-Limit` holding the maximum request limit and `X-Rate-Limit-Duration` holding the rate-limiter duration. These are signals to the client to back off with requests.

Rate limiting can be used to defend against some types of attacks. For example, a normal user will not be able to submit login credentials more than a couple of times per second. If you see many rapid consecutive login attempts, your service is likely under attack by a malicious script trying to guess the password; rate limiting can guard against such a brute-force effort. However, rate limiting can be a double-edged sword, because it doesn't distinguish between legitimate and malicious traffic. When your site is experiencing a denial of service (DoS) or distributed denial of service (DDoS) attack, although you can use rate limiting to avoid your server getting overloaded, you'll be turning away legitimate traffic as well because a simple rate-limiting system controls only the overall traffic flow.

Some advanced rate-limiting policies, such as constraining only unauthorized requests (by checking for the existence of an authorization header, for instance), can provide better defense against DDoS attacks. We'd be more than happy if security experts in the community can help us to further improve the rate-limiting middleware.

When it comes to security, we want to be open and frank about it. In the preceding discussions, we've touched on how Dapr can help with certain aspects of security now, how it likely will be able to help in the future, and some areas where help from the community will be needed to make further improvements. The rest of the chapter covers in more detail what Dapr offers today. Because Dapr is under rapid development, please consult the online documentation (*https://oreil.ly/bF23s*) for the latest security feature updates.

Dapr Security Features

At the time of writing, Dapr provides a handful of security features, including secret stores, a secret API, and mutual TLS.

Secret Stores

Secret stores are designed to store sensitive information such as certificates and passwords. The difference between a database and a secret store is that a secret store applies additional mechanisms and constraints to further protect the saved information, such as:

Constrained API surface and access control
A secret store often requires specific credentials and server roles.

Encryption at rest
Some secret stores automatically encrypt secret data at rest with a store-controlled key or a user-supplied key. Note that the Kubernetes secret store saves secrets as base-64 encoded data in the underlying etcd store. The data by default is not encrypted, but you can opt in to encryption at rest. See the Kubernetes documentation (*https://oreil.ly/KmVD-*) for more details.

Hardware protection
Security stores like Azure Key Vault use hardware security modules (HSMs) to safeguard secrets using specialized hardware.

As with other components, Dapr supports pluggable secret stores through a secret store interface. At the time of writing, Dapr supports the following secret stores:

- Kubernetes secret store
- Azure Key Vault

- HashiCorp Vault
- AWS Secrets Manager
- Google Cloud KMS
- Google Secret Manager

Dapr offers built-in support for the Kubernetes secret store, so no specific configuration is needed to set that up. Other secret stores can be described by secret store description manifests. For example, the following manifest describes an Azure Key Vault:

```
apiVersion: dapr.io/v1alpha1
kind: Component
metadata:
  name: azurekeyvault
spec:
  type: secretstores.azure.keyvault
  metadata:
  - name: vaultName
    value: "<your key vault name>"
  - name: spnTenantId
    value: "<your service principal tenant ID>"
  - name: spnClientId
    value: "<your service principal app ID>"
  - name: spnCertificateFile
    value : "<pfx certificate file local path>"
```

Once you've defined an Azure Key Vault, you can use Azure tools such as the Azure CLI to store secrets in it. The following sample Azure CLI command creates a secret named redisPassword in an Azure Key Vault:

```
az keyvault secret set --name redisPassword --vault-name <your key vault name>
--value "<your Redis password>"
```

Then when you define other components, you can reference the secrets in your secret store by using a secretKeyRef element. The following sample component manifest defines a Redis state store. The password of the store is saved in Azure Key Vault as a redisPassword secret and is referenced by a secretKeyRef element:

```
apiVersion: dapr.io/v1alpha1
kind: Component
metadata:
  name: statestore
spec:
  type: state.redis
  metadata:
  - name: redisHost
    value: "redis-master:6379"
  - name: redisPassword
    secretKeyRef:
      name: redisPassword
```

```
auth:
    secretStore: azurekeyvault
```

Dapr's secret store feature was designed for Dapr internal usage only. Later, our customers requested a secret API through which application code can access saved secrets. We'll introduce this API shortly.

It's unlikely you'll need to implement a secret store yourself. But in case you do, the following section provides a brief introduction.

Implementing a Secret Store

Dapr defines a secret store as a simple interface that contains an `Init` method and a `GetSecret` method, as shown in the following code snippet:

```
type SecretStore interface {
    Init(metadata Metadata) error
    GetSecret(req GetSecretRequest) (GetSecretResponse, error)
}
```

The `GetSecretRequest` struct contains a key and a collection of key/value pairs that are attached to the request as metadata:

```
type GetSecretRequest struct {
    Name     string              `json:"name"`
    Metadata map[string]string `json:"metadata"`
}
```

Dapr doesn't interpret the metadata in any way. Instead, it simply passes all attached metadata to the secret store implementation. This design is to handle cases in which a secret store requires more information than a secret key name to access a secret. Requesting such metadata makes the code using your security store less portable. Although other stores can choose to ignore the metadata and function as usual, the same metadata keys may be accidentally chosen by multiple secret stores and will be interpreted differently by different stores, causing unpredictable errors. It's highly recommended that you capture enough information in the `Init` method so secrets can be retrieved by secret key name only.

The `GetSecretResponse` struct holds a key/value pair of secret data:

```
type GetSecretResponse struct {
    Data map[string]string `json:"data"`
}
```

If the requested key is not found, your code should return an `error` object.

As previously noted, when you define any Dapr manifest you can use the `secret KeyRef` element to reference secrets. Dapr has also introduced a secret API that allows applications to access secrets through code. We'll introduce this API in the next section.

The Secret API

Dapr exposes a secret API that an application can use to retrieve a secret from a secret store at the endpoint `v1.0/secrets/<secret store name>/<secret key name>`.

This convenient API makes it easy for an application to retrieve secrets and use them in its code. The idea is to help developers avoid saving sensitive information, such as passwords and connection strings, in their code. The API is read-only, which means application code can't create or update any secret keys through it. On the other hand, operations can update the secrets as needed by directly making changes to the secret stores without affecting the code. For example, they can rotate certificates, update passwords, and modify the connection string to a database account with the appropriate access privileges.

Ironically, the downside of this API is exactly its convenience. Once configured, application code can request any secret keys without authentication. As mentioned earlier, under the sidecar architecture, the Dapr sidecar and the application code are considered to be in the same security domain. Hence, allowing direct accesses to the secrets is not necessarily the wrong design. However, there is a potential danger: if application code is compromised, the adversary can gain access to all the secrets in the secret store.

With integration with service identities (see "Identity" on page 80), Dapr is able to offer some automatic authentication and authorization mechanisms to constrain access to secrets. For example, it can enforce a policy that grants an application access only to a particular secret store or even specific secret keys. Then, even when an application is compromised, the attacker won't be able to use the application to gain access to the secrets of other applications sharing the same secret store.

That's about all Dapr provides in terms of secret management. Next, we'll shift gears and talk about how Dapr secures Dapr-to-Dapr communications through mutual TLS.

Mutual TLS (mTLS)

Transport Layer Security (TLS), which replaces the deprecated Secure Sockets Layer (SSL) protocol, is a cryptographic protocol used for secure communication between clients and servers. By default, TLS proves the server's identity to the client using a server X.509 certificate. Optionally, it can also prove the client's identity to the server using a client X.509 certificate. This is called *mutual TLS*. Mutual TLS (mTLS) is often used in distributed systems because in such systems it's hard to identify a server or a client. Instead, components call each other in a mesh, so any component can be both a server and a client. Mutual TLS ensures all service calls among components are authenticated on both sides by cross-checking the certificates.

Before introducing how mTLS works, we need to provide a brief explanation of certificates and related concepts. If you are familiar with these concepts already, you can skip the following subsections.

X.509 certificates

An X.509 certificate is a digital certificate using the international X.509 public key infrastructure (PKI) standard. A certificate is issued by a trusted certificate authority (CA) and contains information about the represented entity such as the verified entity name and validity period of the certificate. A certificate also includes the entity's public key and a signature that has been encoded with the entity's private key. The PKI standard guarantees that if you can use the public key to decrypt the data, the information has been encrypted with the data owner's private key.

When you use your browser to access a site through HTTPS, your browser validates the server's certificate, checking that the certificate was issued by a trusted CA and that the domain name contained in the certificate matches with the address you are trying to access. If both checks pass, the browser displays some visual hint (such as the green padlock shown in Figure 4-2) to indicate you are securely connected to a legitimate server.

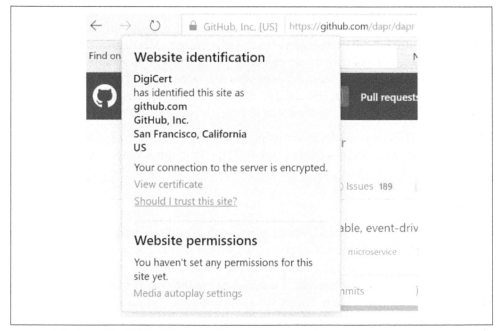

Figure 4-2. A verified HTTPS connection

If the certificate check fails, a modern browser is likely to warn you that your connection to the server is not secure. Figure 4-3 shows an example of a failed certificate check. In this case, the certificate associated with *www.test.com* has expired (the screenshot was captured on February 29, 2020), and hence the certificate check has failed.

 Always access websites through HTTPS, and always check if their certificates are valid. This will help you to avoid some phishing attacks, in which an adversary uses a decoy website that mimics a legitimate website to try to trick you into providing your personal information (bank account or credit card number, email address, password, etc.) to the attacker. When you access a web service in your application code, make sure your code uses HTTPS as well. Similarly, when you expose a public service, always make sure it exposes an HTTPS endpoint, and keep your certificate up to date.

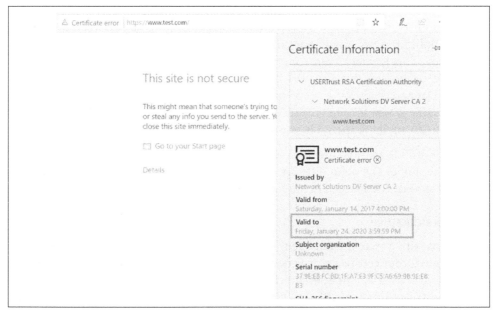

Figure 4-3. An unverified HTTPS connection

A CA is identified by a certificate as well. The certificate is imported into the certificate stores on your computer. There can be multiple levels of CA; an authority without a parent is called a *root CA*. Certificates representing the root CAs are imported to the *Trusted Root Certificate Authorities* store. A child CA needs an issuer certificate from its parent CA to issue new certificates. These certificates are chained together, with the root certificate issued by the root CA. When validating a certificate, you need to trace through the certificate chain until you reach a validated root certificate.

Requesting an X.509 certificate

To request a certificate from a CA, the requestor first generates a public/private key pair. Then it creates a certificate signing request (CSR), which contains its public key and requested fields, such as domain name. It signs the CSR with its own private key and sends the CSR to the CA. The CA verifies the CSR using the requestor's public key. Then it generates a digital certificate that contains the requested fields, the requestor's public key, and the CA's public key. The digital certificate is signed with the CA's private key and sent back to the requestor.

Now that you have an understanding of certificates, we can move on to Dapr mTLS.

Dapr mTLS

Mutual TLS requires each party to identify itself with a certificate, and to obtain a certificate you need to work with a trusted CA. Setting up a CA and completing the certificate application process is not complicated, but it's something developers don't often enjoy. This is where Dapr comes in. It hosts a CA service itself, it automates the certificate generation process, and it establishes a secure communication channel between Dapr sidecars. When your application code uses Dapr sidecars to communicate, all traffic is sent through the secured HTTPS channel automatically, without you needing to do anything special in your code.

The Dapr mTLS architecture is designed to work in both Kubernetes mode and standalone mode. The main difference between the two modes is where the root certificate is stored, as explained in the following section.

Dapr mTLS architecture

Dapr ships with a system component named Sentry that acts as a CA. The CA takes a user-supplied root certificate or generates a self-signed certificate as the root certificate. When a new Dapr sidecar launches, the root certificate is injected into the sidecar as the trusted root certificate. Then the Dapr sidecar requests a new workload certificate from Sentry. Finally, two Dapr sidecars authenticate with each other with corresponding workload certificates. Figure 4-4 illustrates how the whole process works, and the steps are described here in a little more detail:

1. Optionally, an operator loads a root certificate into the Kubernetes secret store (in Kubernetes mode) or a filesystem.
2. Sentry reads the user-supplied root certificate or, if necessary, generates a self-signed certificate as the root certificate itself. When the root certificate is

replaced, Sentry automatically picks up the new certificate and rebuilds the trust chain.

3. When the sidecar injector injects a Dapr sidecar, it retrieves the root certificate and injects it into the Dapr sidecar.

4. When the Dapr sidecar initializes, it checks if mutual TLS is enabled. If so, it sends a CSR to Sentry. Sentry issues a workload certificate that is good for 24 hours, with 15 minutes of allowed clock skew by default. The clock skew allowance is to avoid certificate validation errors because of clock drift.

5. Dapr sidecars use workload certificates to authenticate with each other to establish a secured, encrypted communication channel.

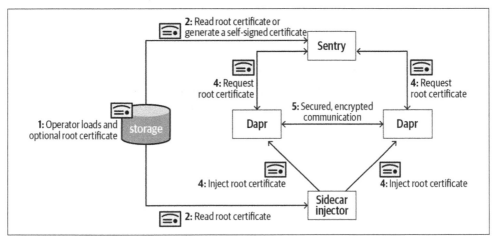

Figure 4-4. Dapr's mutual TLS architecture

Configuring Sentry

Sentry configuration is described by a Dapr configuration file that looks something like this:

```
apiVersion: dapr.io/v1alpha1
kind: Configuration
metadata:
  name: default
spec:
  mtls:
    enabled: true
    workloadCertTTL: "24h"
    allowedClockSkew: "15m"
```

When running in Kubernetes mode, you can use kubectl to view and update Dapr configurations:

```
kubectl get configurations/<configuration name> --namespace <Dapr namespace>
-o yaml
kubectl edit configurations/<configuration name> --namespace <Dapr namespace>
```

Then delete the Sentry pod so that the replacement pod can pick up the new configuration:

```
kubectl delete pod --selector=app=dapr-sentry --namespace <Dapr namespace>
```

When running in standalone mode, you can launch the Sentry process with the --issuer-certificate switch to load a root certificate, and use the --config switch to load a custom configuration file:

```
./sentry --issuer-credentials $HOME/.dapr/certs --trust-domain cluster.local
--config=./my-config.yaml
```

To launch application code with mTLS enabled, you need to supply a Dapr configuration file with mTLS enabled:

```
dapr run --app-id myapp --config ./mtls-config.yaml node myapp.js
```

Dapr mTLS provides secure communication channels between Dapr sidecars. It hides the complexity of certificate management from developers.

Summary

At the time of writing Dapr provides a basic set of security features, including secret management, a secret API, and mutual TLS support. Some additional security features are on the horizon, and we'd be happy to hear your feedback and get contributions.

This concludes our discussion of the fundamentals of Dapr. The rest of the book will focus on various application scenarios and design patterns using Dapr.

CHAPTER 5

Actors

Among the many programming models known today in computer science, the actor model is a prominent one. As you'll learn in this chapter, Dapr provides an efficient, lightweight, and flexible implementation of this programming model that supports any modern programming language.

The Actor Pattern

In computer science, the actor model is described as a mathematical model for concurrent computations. An actor can be thought of as a primitive for these computations: it receives a message and can then make local decisions based on that. An actor encapsulates its own state and achieves scalability by being partitioned using unique IDs. Once it has received a message, an actor can respond to the message, connect to an external system, or create more actors of different types. An actor may be stateful or stateless: when stateful, it modifies its own internal state. This leads to an object-oriented programming experience, where the state of an object is encapsulated within it, modified by strongly typed methods. Actors are always invoked in a turn-based concurrency model and allow for a single-threaded access to any given instance of an actor.

For example, Figure 5-1 illustrates that two concurrent calls to the same actor instance of type `Cat`, invoking the `Eat` method, will execute in a serial manner.

As you can see, each time a request comes in to an actor, a lock is acquired; only then can the method be executed and the actor's state changed. Each actor instance keeps its own state and can change the state of other actors by interacting with them via well-known methods that encapsulate the state-changing logic.

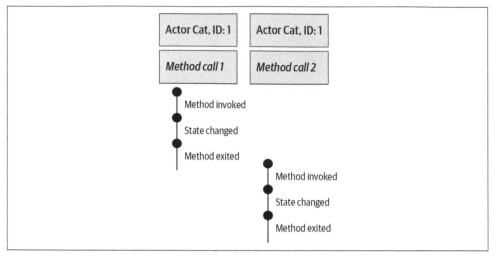

Figure 5-1. Turn-based actor execution

The actor model is nothing new: it was invented in 1973[1] and was inspired by physics and quantum mechanics. Various programming languages were an influence on the actor model, including Lisp and Smalltalk.

The actor model in and of itself does not dictate any special constraints or requirements regarding where the actor runs, its network address, or any other infrastructure concerns. Thus, when invoking an actor, it's the responsibility of the client to know where the actor is placed (for example, on which node, and what the physical network address of that node is). Two instances of the same actor ID cannot exist at the same time; this would be a violation of the actor model and enable a possible corruption of state.

Over the past decades, several actor frameworks have been created to support the programming model. The next section gives a brief introduction to some of them.

Modern Actor Frameworks

In recent years, several actor frameworks have been developed for specific language runtimes, helping developers employ actors at scale across nodes in distributed environments. Examples include Akka (*https://akka.io*), a well-known Scala-based actor model with a .NET port; Orleans (*https://oreil.ly/8m1aL*), a C# virtual actors

---

1 Carl Hewitt, Peter Bishop, and Richard Steiger, "A Universal Modular ACTOR Formalism for Artificial Intelligence," in *IJCAI'73: Proceedings of the Third International Joint Conference on Artificial Intelligence* (San Francisco: Morgan Kaufman, 1973), 235–245.

framework, and Reliable Actors, a virtual actors framework that runs on Microsoft Service Fabric.

The main difference between Akka and Orleans and Service Fabric Reliable Actors is that the latter two frameworks both employ virtual actors. This means that when a user is invoking an actor, these frameworks will create an instance of that actor if it doesn't already exist, place it anywhere in the cluster, and resolve its network address on behalf of the user. A developer does not need to know or care where the actor is placed, and just invokes the actor with an ID and the desired method. Here's an example of invoking a Service Fabric Reliable Actor:

```
using System;
using System.Threading.Tasks;
using Microsoft.ServiceFabric.Actors;
using Microsoft.ServiceFabric.Actors.Client;
using HelloWorld.Interfaces;

namespace ActorClient
{
    class Program
    {
        static void Main(string[] args)
        {
            IHelloWorld actor =
              ActorProxy.Create<IHelloWorld>("MyActor",
              new Uri("fabric:/MyApplication/HelloWorldActorService"));
            Task<string> retval = actor.GetHelloWorldAsync();
            Console.Write(retval.Result);
            Console.ReadLine();
        }
    }
}
```

As you can see, an actor reference is created with a proxy for an actor with ID MyAc tor. The next line invokes an actor method and prints out the result. This concept is similar in many actor frameworks: it usually involves creating a reference to an actor of a given type with an ID, and then invoking a method on that actor.

Reliable Actors support C# and Java and are tied to the underlying hosting platform, Service Fabric. Orleans uses the concept of *silos* to host *grains* (the equivalent of an actor), and silos can be run in any environment that is supported by .NET. Akka runs as a JVM process, accessible to Java/Scala natively and to .NET applications through a .NET port. Akka can run in any environment, including inside containers.

While these modern frameworks all offer the programming experience of actors, they are thus constrained to a limited number of programming languages and/or hosting platforms (in the case of Service Fabric Reliable Actors).

The actor programming model is a very intuitive model, and the concept of encapsulating state and actions as an isolated unit resonates well with people who are familiar with the object-oriented programming (OOP) paradigm. However, if one is not careful with subtle implications of the programming model, it could be misused, as summarized in the next section.

Misuse of the Actor Model

In many cases actors can be used incorrectly, bringing about undesired results. For example, consider the following scenario, where actors are being used to model cars on the road. Each car keeps its own state: in this case, the speed at which it is driving.

At first, the actor model seems like a great fit: an actor is created when a car starts to drive, and when the speed changes, the ChangeSpeed(speed) method is invoked on the actor to update the current state. But then a new requirement creeps into the backlog—the developers need to be able to create a snapshot of the state of all the currently driving cars at any given moment. Their first impulse might be to query each actor (for every car) and aggregate the data from all actors.

However, this creates the following problems:

- Trying to invoke hundreds or thousands of actors simultaneously is a slow, nonperformant operation.
- Querying for the actor state blocks the actors on other calls coming in to update the speed of the vehicles, essentially pausing all of the actor instances active at that moment.

Another common misuse of the actor model is to save large amounts of data with each actor. The larger the data is, the longer it will take for the I/O call invoking the actor (whether getting the state or having the actor save the state) to finish, thereby locking the actor for longer periods and creating bottlenecks. Thus, it becomes clear that it is important to make sure actors fit the problem at hand, and that the problem can be modeled to correctly partition actors so as to not create bottlenecks by invoking a single actor ID from many clients, or saving large amounts of data and slowing down network operations.

If an aggregate view of the data of multiple actors is needed, it is best to query the underlying state store. If that is not viable, it is recommended to have each actor save its data to an external database, which can be queried and provide aggregations. Figure 5-2 illustrates how such queries can be used to aggregate actor states. Chapter 7 will introduce some ideas about making actor aggregation a native actor feature.

Now that you've had a brief overview of the actor programming model and of some common antipatterns in actor programming, let's explore how Dapr implements this programming model.

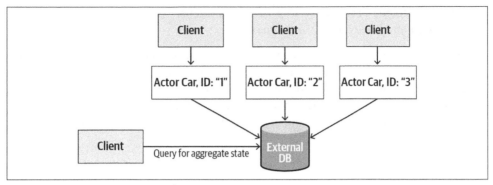

Figure 5-2. Direct state query for aggregate state

Dapr and Actors

Dapr offers a cloud native, resilient, platform-agnostic virtual actors model as part of its core capabilities. The actor runtime runs inside the Dapr runtime, making it easy to write language-specific actor SDKs on top of Dapr, while making actors invokable from any language via HTTP or gRPC.

At the time of writing, Dapr also supports writing actors in .NET and Java with Dapr SDKs. A Python SDK is under active development.

When we decided to support the actor model, we could have chosen an existing framework. However, we opted to write an entirely new actor framework because we saw two demands that weren't met by existing frameworks:

- The need for a language-agnostic actor model
- The need for an actor model that runs natively on Kubernetes, but is independent and can run on a local developer machine just as well

With that in mind, we've decided to tackle some of the hardest problems of virtual actors: the activation of actors across a cluster at scale while ensuring single activation for any given actor ID, single-threaded access, fast performance, and advanced features such as timers and persistent reminders.

The actor functionality in Dapr resides in two places: inside the Dapr runtime and in a system service called the *placement service*. The placement service is in charge of discovering new hosts for actors across the cluster. Once a host is connected to the placement service via a streaming gRPC connection, the host uses a consistent hashing algorithm to construct a map of the actor types hosted on that host.

The specific algorithm used by Dapr is called *consistent hashing with bounded loads*; it was first released by Google in a whitepaper (*https://oreil.ly/nkXJu*) from 2016. This algorithm performs particularly well in environments where nodes (actor hosts in our case) join and leave quickly and dynamically.

Since Dapr runs as a sidecar, in Kubernetes the host would be a pod, not a node. Pods can be moved between nodes, destroyed, or upgraded, and when a deployment is scaled out, thousands of pods can join while their earlier instances are removed. In this kind of dynamic environment, the hashing algorithm has to be fast and performant, and it must shift as few of the actors as possible between hosts when the ring (combination of hosts) changes.

Figure 5-3 shows how the placement service works in Dapr. First the hosts establish a connection to the placement service, reporting their address, health, and hosted actor types.

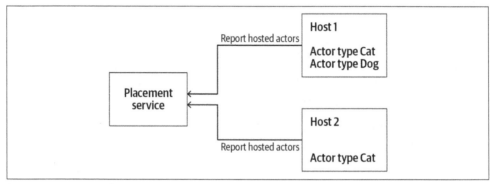

Figure 5-3. Dapr placement service

The placement service then constructs a hash table that consists of an array of hosts for a given actor type. Every time the hash table is updated, the placement service updates all the Dapr sidecars that are connected to it, as illustrated in Figure 5-4.

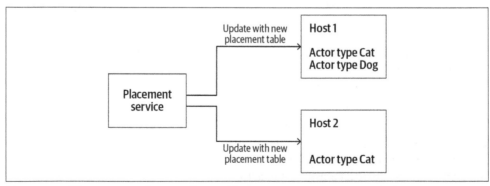

Figure 5-4. Placement updates to Dapr sidecars

When a call from a client comes in to a Dapr sidecar to invoke an actor, the local side-car instance looks up the address of the actor in the hash table. The hash table receives as input the actor type and ID and returns the address for that actor. The following code from the Dapr runtime shows this:

```
func (a *actorsRuntime) lookupActorAddress(actorType, actorID string) string {
    // read lock for table map
    a.placementTableLock.RLock()
    defer a.placementTableLock.RUnlock()

    t := a.placementTables.Entries[actorType]
    if t == nil {
        return ""
    }
    host, err := t.GetHost(actorID)
    if err != nil || host == nil {
        return ""
    }
    return fmt.Sprintf("%s:%v", host.Name, host.Port)
}
```

As seen here, a read lock is placed on the placement table. A list of entries is retrieved, with the key being the actor type, and then a host is polled for the specific actor ID. The consistent hashed table will return the host under whose range this actor ID falls. Finally, the network address of the host is returned.

The placement service has a difficult job: it needs to keep all the Dapr sidecars in the cluster synced with the latest snapshot of the table whenever new hosts join or leave. Syncing is important, as otherwise multiple activations of the same actor instance can occur. To do this, Dapr uses a unique three-phase commit to update the sidecars. When a new host joins and a shift in the hash table occurs, Dapr will issue a "lock" command to all of the sidecars. After this command is issued, ongoing requests to actors are allowed to finish, while incoming requests are held on the fly. After receiving confirmation from all participating sidecars that they have been locked, an update with the new hash table commences. The Dapr sidecars each receive the new hash table and update their local copy.

The third and final stage is to unlock the sidecars. This process ensures that all new requests in all Dapr instances are working against the same copy of the hash table. The following code from the placement service shows this:

```
func (p *Service) PerformTablesUpdate(hosts
        []daprinternal_pb.PlacementService_ReportDaprStatusServer,
        options placementOptions) {
    p.updateLock.Lock()
    defer p.updateLock.Unlock()

    if options.incrementGeneration {
        p.generation++
```

```
    }

    o := daprinternal_pb.PlacementOrder{
        Operation: "lock",
    }

    for _, host := range hosts {
        err := host.Send(&o)
        if err != nil {
            log.Errorf("error updating host on lock operation: %s", err)
            continue
        }
    }

    v := fmt.Sprintf("%v", p.generation)

    o.Operation = "update"
    o.Tables = &daprinternal_pb.PlacementTables{
        Version: v,
        Entries: map[string]*daprinternal_pb.PlacementTable{},
    }

    for k, v := range p.entries {
        hosts, sortedSet, loadMap, totalLoad := v.GetInternals()
        table := daprinternal_pb.PlacementTable{
            Hosts:     hosts,
            SortedSet: sortedSet,
            TotalLoad: totalLoad,
            LoadMap:   make(map[string]*daprinternal_pb.Host),
        }

        for lk, lv := range loadMap {
            h := daprinternal_pb.Host{
                Name: lv.Name,
                Load: lv.Load,
                Port: lv.Port,
            }
            table.LoadMap[lk] = &h
        }
        o.Tables.Entries[k] = &table
    }

    for _, host := range hosts {
        err := host.Send(&o)
        if err != nil {
            log.Errorf("error updating host on update operation: %s", err)
            continue
        }
    }

    o.Tables = nil
    o.Operation = "unlock"
```

```
        for _, host := range hosts {
            err := host.Send(&o)
            if err != nil {
                log.Errorf("error updating host on unlock operation: %s", err)
                continue
            }
        }
    }
```

If a node crashes during the lock phase it is taken out of the ring, and upon rejoining it will receive the latest snapshot before taking in any new actor client requests.

Now let's switch to the user's perspective and learn how to use Dapr actors.

Invoking a Dapr Actor

To invoke a Dapr actor, you can use either HTTP or gRPC to talk to the Dapr API. The following example shows how to invoke a Dapr actor over HTTP:

```
curl -X POST http://localhost:3500/v1.0/actors/stormtrooper/50/method/shoot
```

This example uses curl to invoke Dapr running on port 3500. It invokes an actor of type stormtrooper with ID 50 and a method named shoot. The same can be done with any of the Dapr proto clients. This capability is unique to Dapr: it allows a developer to invoke a Dapr actor written in any language using any programming language that understands HTTP.

Next, we'll examine how Dapr actors manage state.

State Management

Dapr uses external state stores to save the state of actors. This gives the following benefits:

- Visibility into actor data
- Ability to query the underlying store for aggregate data
- Flexibility to use a variety of on-premise/cloud-based databases

The third benefit in particular plays well with the cloud native aspect of Dapr, allowing developers to run actors in resource-constrained environments using a state store like Redis and then, when running in the cloud, to take advantage of cloud databases that offer higher service-level agreements (SLAs) and easier maintenance. This allows developers to port their applications between environments and embrace a variety of programming languages.

Dapr constructs the key for an actor's state using the following pattern:

```
<DAPR-ID>||<ACTOR-TYPE>||<ACTOR-ID>||<KEY>
```

where:

- *<DAPR-ID>* represents the unique ID given to the Dapr application.
- *<ACTOR-TYPE>* represents the type of the actor.
- *<ACTOR-ID>* represents the unique ID of the actor instance for an actor type.
- *<KEY>* is a key for the specific state value. An actor ID can hold multiple state keys.

Knowing this, it's easy to query for the state of a given actor or perform aggregate queries for the state of multiple actors, if the underlying store supports a SQL interface. State is saved in a transactional manner, and Dapr allows actors to save granular state using specific keys. For example, a `Cat` actor might save a state value for the key `meal`, a different state value for `color`, and another state value for `sleeping`. Then, when an actor needs to have its state restored, it can be lazily loaded and not restored all at once. Similarly, when saving state, this reduces latency and increases throughput as only the granular state is saved, not a single data structure containing all the values.

Like in some other actor frameworks, Dapr actors can be triggered by either external calls or internal signals triggered by timers and reminders. We'll look at how this works next.

Timers

Timers are a way to schedule specific work on a given timetable for an actor. When an actor is triggered by a timer, it can change its state. Timers are not persisted and will not be invoked when an actor fails over to a different host or gets reactivated after garbage collection. Whenever an actor is activated, it has the responsibility to reregister the timers.

The following example shows how to create an actor timer via HTTP:

```
curl http://localhost:3500/v1.0/actors/stormtrooper/50/timers/checkRebels \
    -H "Content-Type: application/json"
-d '{
    "data": "someData",
    "dueTime": "1m",
    "period": "20s",
    "callback": "myEventHandler"
}'
```

This example invokes the actor type `stormtrooper` with ID `50` and creates a new timer called `checkRebels`. In the HTTP POST body sent to the Dapr runtime, we can see that data is attached to the call. That data will be passed to the actor instance when the timer fires. The `dueTime` attribute is the initial timeout to wait before firing the timer for the first time. The `period` attribute represents the recurring interval for that timer, and `callback` specifies the method on the actor that should be invoked by Dapr. You can also delete a timer on an actor using HTTP:

```
curl http://localhost:3500/v1.0/actors/stormtrooper/50/timers/checkRebels \
    -X "Content-Type: application/json"
```

The following example shows how to register a timer with the Dapr C# actor SDK:

```
{
    using System;
    using System.Threading.Tasks;
    using Dapr.Actors;
    using Dapr.Actors.Runtime;
    using IDemoActorInterface;

    public class DemoActor : Actor, IDemoActor, IRemindable
    {
        private const string StateName = "my_data";
        private IActorReminder reminder;

        /// <summary>
        /// Initializes a new instance of the <see cref="DemoActor"/>
        /// class.
        /// </summary>
        /// <param name="service">Actor service hosting the
        ///     actor.</param>
        /// <param name="actorId">Actor ID.</param>
        public DemoActor(ActorService service, ActorId actorId)
            : base(service, actorId)
        {
        }

        /// <inheritdoc/>
        public Task RegisterTimer()
        {
            return this.RegisterTimerAsync("Test", this.TimerCallBack,
                null, TimeSpan.FromSeconds(5), TimeSpan.FromSeconds(5));
        }

        /// <inheritdoc/>
        public Task UnregisterTimer()
        {
            return this.UnregisterTimerAsync("Test");
        }

        private Task TimerCallBack(object data)
        {
            // Code for timer callback can be added here.
            return Task.CompletedTask;
        }
    }
}
```

This example uses the `RegisterTimer` method to register a new timer called `Test`, have it wait five seconds before it first fires, and then fire again every five seconds. The callback function is `TimerCallback`. When an actor dies, the timer will not invoke it again unless the actor is instantiated again.

Reminders work similarly to timers, but they are persistent. They don't die off along with the actor instance. Instead, they always exist unless explicitly unregistered, as explained in the next section.

Reminders

Unlike timers, reminders are persistent. They are used to schedule a recurring piece of work at a specified interval. If an actor dies or relocates to a different host, the reminder is persisted and will invoke (and thus recreate the actor) when it fires. The following example shows how to create an actor reminder using HTTP:

```
curl http://localhost:3500/v1.0/actors/stormtrooper/50/reminders/checkRebels \
    -H "Content-Type: application/json"
-d '{
    "data": "someData",
    "dueTime": "1m",
    "period": "20s"
}'
```

This example creates a `checkRebels` reminder on an actor of type `stormtrooper` with ID `50`. The data that's passed to the Dapr runtime includes `dueTime`, meaning the first timeout to wait before starting the reminder, and `period`, which sets the recurring interval.

You can explicitly delete a reminder using an HTTP request. The following example shows how to delete the `checkRebels` reminder:

```
curl http://localhost:3500/v1.0/actors/stormtrooper/50/reminders/checkRebels \
    -X "Content-Type: application/json"
```

The following example shows how to create a reminder using the Dotnet SDK:

```
public class DemoActor : Actor, IDemoActor, IRemindable
{
    private const string StateName = "my_data";
    private IActorReminder reminder;

    public DemoActor(ActorService service, ActorId actorId)
            : base(service, actorId)
    {
    }
    /// <inheritdoc/>
    public async Task RegisterReminder()
    {
        this.reminder = await this.RegisterReminderAsync("Test",
```

```
            null, TimeSpan.FromSeconds(5), TimeSpan.FromSeconds(5));
    }

    /// <inheritdoc/>
    public Task UnregisterReminder()
    {
        return this.UnregisterReminderAsync("Test");
    }

    /// <inheritdoc/>
    public Task ReceiveReminderAsync(string reminderName, byte[]
        state, TimeSpan dueTime, TimeSpan period)
    {
        // This method is invoked when an actor reminder is fired.
        return Task.CompletedTask;
    }
}
```

Now that you've learned the basic components and features of Dapr actors, let's close the chapter with a complete example using the Dapr .NET SDK.

Getting Started with Writing Dapr Actors for C#

To get started with Dapr actors for C#, first download and install Dapr (*https:// oreil.ly/VISmr*) on your machine. You're also going to need the .NET Core SDK. The full tutorial is available on GitHub (*https://oreil.ly/dekIm*).

Defining the Actor Interface

To program in the actor programming model using the C# SDKs, the first thing you need to do is define the interface your actor will implement. We'll define an interface here:

```
namespace IDemoActorInterface
{
    using System.Threading.Tasks;
    using Dapr.Actors;

    /// <summary>
    /// Interface for Actor method.
    /// </summary>
    public interface IDemoActor : IActor
    {
        /// <summary>
        /// Method to save data.
        /// </summary>
        /// <param name="data">Data to save.</param>
        /// <returns>A task that represents the asynchronous save
        ///    operation.</returns>
        Task SaveData(MyData data);
```

```
/// <summary>
/// Data used by the sample actor.
/// </summary
public class MyData
{
    /// <summary>
    /// Gets or sets the value for PropertyA.
    /// </summary>
    public string PropertyA { get; set; }
}
}
```

You can see that our actor has one method, SaveData, which accepts a class of type MyData. This class encapsulates the state for every actor activated with an ID.

Implementing the Actor Interface

The next step is to implement the interface:

```
namespace DaprDemoActor
{
    using System;
    using System.Threading.Tasks;
    using Dapr.Actors;
    using Dapr.Actors.Runtime;
    using IDemoActorInterface;

    /// </summary>
    public class DemoActor : Actor, IDemoActor, IRemindable
    {
        private const string StateName = "my_data";
        private IActorReminder reminder;

        /// <summary>
        /// Initializes a new instance of the <see cref="DemoActor"/> class.
        /// </summary>
        /// <param name="service">Actor service hosting the actor.</param>
        /// <param name="actorId">Actor ID.</param>
        public DemoActor(ActorService service, ActorId actorId)
            : base(service, actorId)
        {
        }

        /// <inheritdoc/>
        public async Task SaveData(MyData data)
        {
            Console.WriteLine($"This is Actor id {this.Id} with data
            {data.ToString()}");
            /// Set state using StateManager. State is saved after the method
            /// execution.
            await this.StateManager.SetStateAsync<MyData>(StateName, data);
        }
```

```
        }
    }
```

The `DemoActor` class implements the `IDemoActor` interface and inherits from the `Actor` base class, coming from the `Dapr.Actors` namespace.

Behind the scenes the Dapr Dotnet SDK launches, registers the actor type, and then contacts the Dapr runtime and registers itself as a host for the `DemoActor` actor type. The Dapr runtime then updates the placement service, which in turn updates the actors hash table and sends it to all the Dapr sidecars in the clusters. Whenever the `SaveData` method gets called, the `StateManager` is invoked with `SetStateAsync`. This method saves the data according to a specific key—in this example, it's `"my_data"`.

Summary

Dapr provides a new actor framework that supports all modern programming languages and typical virtual actor behaviors such as turn-based concurrency, state management, timers, and reminders. If you have previous experience with existing virtual actor frameworks, you'll find using Dapr actors a very familiar process.

A key difference in Dapr's actor design is that Dapr treats actor instances not as independent processes but as routing rules on the same web service. This allows Dapr to host actor instances with high density—we experimented with launching a million actor instances on a single node without much trouble.

In the next chapter, you'll see a couple of examples of how actors can be used in some application scenarios. And in the final chapter, you'll see how we envision some new and advanced features of Dapr actors.

CHAPTER 6

Application Patterns

Dapr is designed to support cloud native applications. In this chapter we will first review what it means to be "cloud native," and then we'll discuss how Dapr can help you migrate your on-premises applications to the cloud. After that, we'll examine Dapr in broader contexts such as tooling integration, system integration application, and edge computing.

Cloud Native Applications

Mount Everest is the highest mountain on Earth. With an elevation of 29,029 feet (8,848 meters), it brings extreme challenges to climbers through a combination of freezing temperatures, high solar radiation, dangerous terrain, and low oxygen levels in the air. Most climbers need supplemental oxygen and tons of professional climbing gear to help them cope with the harsh environment. However, even under such extreme conditions, we can still find a few native survivors, such as the snow leopard, the Himalayan black bear, and the Himalayan tahr. Although they are endangered species now (because of human influences, not the environment itself), they've been roaming the mountain for thousands of years more than humans have.

When we talk about cloud native applications, we're referring to applications that are specifically designed for the cloud environment. When you lift and shift an application to the cloud, you have to make sure it has what it needs to survive—like the oxygen tank needed to climb Everest. Infrastructure as a Service (IaaS) offers a simulated on-premises environment for the application. It allows your application to function in the cloud (an oxygen-deprived environment) as if it was in an on-premises (oxygen-rich) environment. However, to fully take advantage of the benefits of the cloud—such as per-second billing, dynamic scaling, and seamless failover—your application needs to be able to *adapt* to the cloud environment so that it can roam around and thrive without life support.

To understand how to design a cloud native application, you first need to understand how the cloud environment differs from an on-premises environment.

Cloud Environment

Cloud platforms manage servers, and your on-premises datacenters manage servers. The mission in both cases is to keep the infrastructure available for applications. So how does the cloud environment differ from the on-premises environment? A cloud environment is distinct in two ways: embracing errors and horizontal scale.

Embracing errors

In a local datacenter, a server crashing is a bad day for IT staff but a good day for developers—it's an unexpected break from work. Because the mean time to recovery (MTTR) of a failing server is often quite high, IT folks keep tight control over the servers and implement ironclad policies to ensure their stability and maintain high availability.

The cloud is a rather different environment. A regular cloud datacenter often holds hundreds of thousands of physical servers hosting even more virtualized servers. Even a 1% error rate means there will be hundreds or even thousands of servers failing on any given day. And your workload could be on one of those failed servers. The way the cloud deals with these failures is quite different—instead of fixing a failing server on the spot, it simply allocates you another healthy server from its humongous server pool and expects you to carry on with your business as usual. In such a setting, the MTTR of your application depends almost entirely on how quickly you can migrate your application to the new server and successfully launch it.

Even when servers are not failing, a cloud platform may choose to proactively relocate your application to a different server to optimize resource utilization. For example, when a server is deemed to be too busy, part of its workload may get evicted to reduce its load. This means your application must be ready to be moved at any time.

To adapt to such an environment, your application must be able to be consistently deployed without human interaction. *Consistency* is the key here, and over the past decades numerous technologies have been developed to achieve that—from installation scripts to installation packages, to virtualization, and eventually containers.

Containers provide a lightweight way to package all the dependencies of an application together with the application itself. This allows an application to be quickly migrated to a different server and launched in a predictable, consistent manor without missing any dependencies. So the success of containers in the cloud era isn't accidental—they offer the key technology for applications to maintain availability in a cloud environment.

Physics tells us that moving and installing a smaller package is faster than dealing with a bigger package. This has inspired the microservices architecture, in which an application is split into smaller, self-contained, loosely coupled components so the individual parts can be moved around more easily.

However, moving one component around should not break communication with other components. Technologies such as service meshes allow such component mobility within a well-controlled compute plane. Architectural choices such as loose coupling allow greater flexibility by replacing direct communications among components with messaging through a robust messaging backbone.

Moving state is even more challenging. It's often said that data has its gravity that pulls applications around it. Dapr in general assumes data is saved in external data stores. In other words, Dapr allows applications to move around these data gravity wells, which are presumably stable and hard to move. We'll discuss a few patterns for state availability later in this chapter.

Horizontal scale

When an application needs more processing power in an on-premises datacenter, the hosting server needs to be upgraded to provide more memory, more disk space, or more CPU power for the application—or the application needs to be migrated to a more capable server and relaunched.

You can perform similar upgrades on IaaS, as cloud platforms are trying to offer more and more powerful machine options to meet the needs of larger applications. However, in doing this you are not taking full advantage of the cloud's elasticity. Elasticity is one of the biggest value propositions of the cloud—it allows you to pay for exactly the amount of compute resources you consume, down to the second. And when you need more processing power, you can recruit as many servers as you can afford. The cloud puts an instance of your application on each of the servers and joins the servers behind a load balancer, which distributes user traffic to all connected servers. With this arrangement, you can theoretically *scale out* to as many server instances as you need and *scale in* to one or even zero instances when you don't have much (or any) traffic to your application.

Scaling out requires your application to be able to be stably deployed and configured on multiple servers, so what we've discussed with regards to embracing errors also applies here—we need to be able to rapidly and stably deploy multiple running instances of an application.

As long as you can get the resources you need to run your application, you shouldn't care that much how and where they're provided. In other words, you don't want to take on any unnecessary burden to manage the underlying infrastructure. This idea is what's at the root of the whole serverless trend.

Now that you're equipped with a good understanding of how a cloud environment is different from traditional datacenters, we can summarize what it takes to design a cloud native application.

Cloud native design

A cloud native application should be designed to embrace errors and to scale horizontally. Experience tells us that applications with the following characteristics adapt better to a cloud environment:

Made up of self-contained, loosely coupled components
> To reduce the possible downtime because of server migrations, your application should be decomposed into smaller pieces that can be deployed individually. And because there is generally no guaranteed ordering to how the components are launched, each component needs to be self-sufficient. It shouldn't crash if some components it depends on become unavailable. Instead, it should wait and resume normal operation when all dependencies are restored.

Message-based integration
> When your application's components run on a controlled compute plane on which they can assume connectivity, they can roam around as needed. This applies to a single cluster or to multiple clusters connected through a private network or a service mesh. If such an assumption doesn't hold, your application's components can use a messaging backbone to connect with each other through messages. As introduced in earlier chapters, message-based integration and event-driven design have lots of benefits. In many cases, message-based design can help to eliminate central pieces that are likely to become bottlenecks of the system. For example, instead of using a central job dispatcher to dispatch jobs to different recipients, you can have a job publisher publishing jobs to a queue, and you can launch as many job processors as needed to drain the queue.

Consistently deployable
> Your application components should be packaged in a package format that can be stably deployed. The package should be self-contained without any assumed external dependencies except for the expected package runtime, such as a container runtime. A package repository is often needed to facilitate package distribution, but other means, such as a file share, can also be used for simple cases.

Observable
> Because your application is made up of mobile components in the cloud, it's often hard to track what's going on when something breaks. Thus, it's desirable for each component to report telemetry and traces to a central data collector so that you can observe the whole system. It's also important that you can correlate data from distributed sources so that you can trace complete call chains.

Isolation from the infrastructure

Although you don't have to design your application to be cloud-agnostic, it's often desirable to create a cushion between your application and the underlying infrastructure. This means not creating direct dependencies on platform-specific services such as state stores, secret stores, and load balancers. Experience tells us that the requirements of an application always evolve. How your application looks in three years might be totally different from what you envision today. You may also face different scale and latency demands and need to address nonfunctional requirement changes, such as if your company forms a partnership with a new service provider. By building a cushion between your application and the underlying infrastructure, you create more flexibility for the application to adapt to such changes. The cushion also allows you to adapt your application to different hosting needs, such as hosting in on-premises datacenters for disconnected scenarios where cloud-based servers are unavailable.

Horizontally scalable

Components in your application should be horizontally scalable. This means a component instance should not assume it's a singleton in the world. If state is shared across instances, your application must account for potential read/write race conditions and be ready to resolve possible conflicts. A better design ensures an instance either doesn't maintain local state or keeps the state encapsulated to itself. This design maximizes the mobility of a component so the component can be easily relocated elsewhere.

Explicit API

In a complex distributed system, many components are designed, implemented, and managed by different teams. It's a good practice to explicitly define the interface to your component as an API—and you should honor that API as a binding contract between your component and any consumers of the component. The API definition covers not only methods but also data contracts. Your API should be explicitly versioned to avoid possible confusion by customers when you evolve the API design. You should request that your peers follow the same API design principles so that your code is not accidentally broken by others because of their volatile API surfaces.

Dapr has been designed with enabling these characteristics in mind. The next section discusses several scenarios in which Dapr assists in developing applications that are well suited to the cloud.

Cloud Native Applications with Dapr

Dapr is a distributed application runtime that is designed to help you build cloud native applications. What's unique about Dapr, however, is that it doesn't mandate that you take a microservices approach from day one. Instead, you can evolve your application at your own pace and get help from Dapr whenever it's needed.

This section first covers how you can evolve a legacy application for the cloud using Dapr. Then it introduces some patterns you can use when designing cloud native applications from scratch using Dapr.

Evolving a monolithic application

Let's start with a monolithic application that has all the logic in one code package and runs as a singleton. It uses an external database to save state, but it also keeps a fair amount of state in memory. It uses Microsoft Active Directory (AD) for authentication. Figure 6-1 shows the application architecture when it runs on premises.

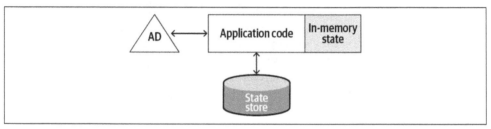

Figure 6-1. A monolithic application

The first thing we'll do is introduce a Dapr sidecar that takes over the in-memory state access. Because Dapr can be configured to use an in-memory Redis state store, doing so introduces only minimal overhead in terms of latency.

Figure 6-2 illustrates the updated architecture with the Dapr sidecar included. The update doesn't affect existing application code that accesses the external state store. Dapr assumes state access to be based on key/value pairs; it doesn't manage the relational database, which is what's likely to be in use here. This demonstrates the nonintrusive nature of Dapr—you can choose to use just the features you need and keep the rest of your code untouched.

This is a small yet significant change—the application code itself becomes stateless. This means the code can be relocated with ease by the cloud platform. As a bonus, the application code can now be containerized to further improve code mobility. When you deploy the newly containerized application to a PaaS platform, perhaps built on top of managed Kubernetes clusters, you get automatic failover and potentially faster deployment times when the container image is cached on cluster nodes.

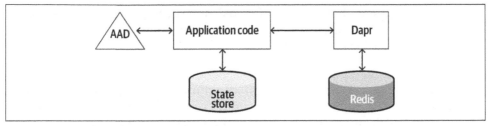

Figure 6-2. Separating in-memory state via Dapr

If you look closely at the figure, you'll see that we smuggled in a little change on the side. We updated Active Directory to Azure Active Directory (AAD). However, the actual switch is a little more complicated than this casual change suggests. Although AAD can be connected to and synced with AD, you can't rely on protocols such as Kerberos anymore; you'll have to adapt your application to use more internet-friendly protocols such as SAML 2.0 and OAuth 2.0. This is just something you have to do when you switch from an on-premises environment to the cloud, unless you deploy your application on a VM that is domain-joined to your existing AD (which is also a possibility).

We haven't touched the core application code yet. As mentioned earlier, the application runs as a singleton, which means it can run only as a single instance. A singleton application often has the following characteristics:

Exclusive access to state
Under the singleton pattern, the application owns the entire state set and has exclusive read/write access to the data store. For example, in a singleton car reservation system, the application can query the database, find an unreserved car, and reserve it for a customer. It doesn't need to worry about someone else coming in and grabbing the car between the time when the query results are returned and the time when the reservation operation can be completed. Of course, a singleton application can support multiple users. In such cases, the application often relies on database transaction isolation to sequentially handle user transactions.

Causal usage of in-memory state
A singleton application can keep in-memory state for better performance. For example, a voting application can keep an in-memory list of leading candidates. Because the singleton application is the only one that reads and writes the in-memory list, it can safely use the in-memory data structure to provide fast access. When we moved the in-memory state behind Dapr, we may have carefully configured Dapr to use strong consistency and a last-write-wins policy to avoid introducing unexpected behaviors. However, it shouldn't have mattered, as the application is a singleton anyway.

When a singleton application crashes and restarts, it can choose to restore its state from the external store under a certain recovery point objective, but some in-flight transactions might be lost.

Global decisions

Because a singleton application knows everything in the application universe, it can make informed decisions at any time. For example, a truck fleet scheduler can calculate the most optimized routes for all trucks in the fleet as it has complete visibility into the entire data set.

Dapr is not a magic pill that can fix everything, however, so at this point in time you need to assess your code and decide if you want to break away from the singleton pattern so that your application can be horizontally scaled. Remaining a singleton, which is a fine design pattern, will certainly be a valid choice in some scenarios.

For the sake of discussion, let's say in this case you do want to break away from the singleton pattern. One thing you can consider is separating the job generation parts of your code from the job handling parts of your code and packaging them as two separate packages. At an abstract level, all systems take in some jobs and process these jobs. The part that takes in jobs usually involves user interactions, while the part that processes jobs can usually run as a backend process. Thus, we can divide the monolithic application into a frontend and a backend. This is also a good place to introduce loose coupling into the system—instead of having the frontend talk directly to the backend, we'll use a job queue in between, as shown in Figure 6-3. This strategy splits up the application where possible and gradually shifts parts of the application to the cloud. This is sometimes called the *strangler pattern*, as the old services are gradually separated out from the monolith into independent microservices.

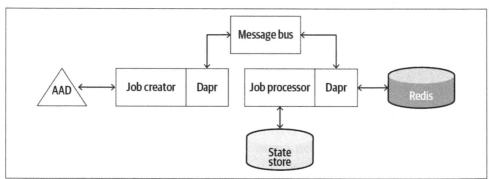

Figure 6-3. Separating the job creation and job processing parts of the application

After the separation, the job creator becomes stateless, as all it does is publish jobs to the job queue through Dapr. This aligns well with the frontend, as the UI is usually stateless and can be scaled out as needed to provide better response times to the users. The backend can be scaled independently based on workload. Of course, if the backend remains a singleton, it will take time to drain the job queue.

What's not shown in the diagram is the feedback to the user. With this design, the interaction between the user and the system is asynchronous—the user doesn't get immediate feedback after submitting a job. A separate channel, such as a message pipeline in the reverse direction, can be used to send feedback to the user.

That's quite a journey, and the application is getting ready to go for cloud scale. However, we can take this a step further. If we encapsulate a job as an actor, we can make a job a self-contained element that can be manipulated by the job processor. We can even attempt to make jobs autonomous—the job processor launches a job actor with a reminder (see Chapter 5) that keeps checking if the job is finished. In such a case, the job processor does nothing but launch a job actor, and all jobs can execute in parallel on all available compute nodes. And while we're at it, we can use Dapr authentication middleware (see Chapter 4) to handle authentication. The updated architecture is shown in Figure 6-4.

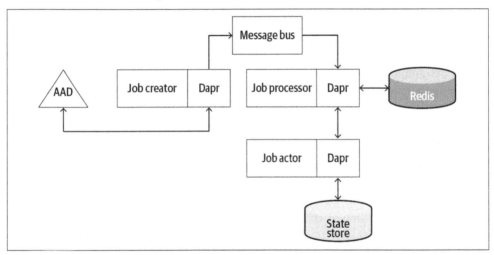

Figure 6-4. Using a job actor

Figure 6-4 also reaches another milestone—the application is detached from the underlying infrastructure. This means the application can be dynamically reconfigured when it's deployed to different environments. That's not always necessary, but it's a great feature to have if you're worried about vendor lock-in.

In this section, we've taken a legacy application and "Daprized" it, as Mark Russinovich would say. Next, let's see how we can design a brand-new cloud native application with Dapr.

Designing a cloud native application

In this part, we'll work on a travel agent website that books vacation travel packages. The website has a public-facing endpoint for individual users. It also provides customized deployments for enterprises to offer an integrated experience with their existing systems, such as accounting and mailing. We'll assume all initial requirement collection work has been finished, and we'll jump directly into designing our first minimum viable product (MVP). We won't be able to discuss all the details involved in designing a new application but will focus instead on the general ideas.

 The most important job of an architect is to correctly draw component boundaries. An experienced architect designs just enough components for the current version while leaving natural extension points for future versions. They'll also consider the structure and capabilities of the engineering team, as well as the long-term goals of the business. This requires technical capability business vision, as well as some artistic touches—which is one reason that good architects are hard to find. Many architects attempt to create flexible architectures by overengineering. A good architect knows when to make subtractions to keep the architecture lean.

When designing a new system, some architects like to first identify the types of entities being managed by the system, including actions that can be taken on these entities. Then they design APIs around the create, read, update, delete (CRUD) actions of the entities. This is a fine approach. However, these actions are not necessarily aligned with user workflows.

Another approach is to start by identifying the different types of users of the system and then design your APIs around their workflows (this is essentially the idea of domain-driven design, or DDD). Grouping the APIs by users is important, as different users may have different entry points, scale factors, authentication requirements, and access policies. It's also prudent to think about having separate read-only APIs and APIs that manipulate entity states, because you can often design additional optimizations for read-only APIs (such as caching and prepopulated views).

When you design applications with Dapr, you can take a hybrid approach—you can model entities in your system as actors and define APIs based on user activities. Let's assume we've identified the following entities in the system:

- Vacation package
  - Flight reservation
  - Car reservation
  - Hotel reservation

- Traveler
  — Profile, such as name, address, and travel budget
  — Payment method
  — Reservations
- Travel policy
- Partners
  — Profile, such as name, contract info, and service type
  — Inventory
  — Special offers and promotions

And we've identified the following users and their typical workflows:

- Administrators
  — Manage travel policies
  — Manage partners
  — Manage vacation packages
  — Manage travelers
- Travelers
  — Book a vacation package
  — Cancel a reservation
- Partners
  — Update inventory
  — Update offers

With these in mind, we can come up with a design with a UI layer, an API layer, and an entity layer, as shown in Figure 6-5. The figure shows that most entities are encapsulated as actors. However, partner inventory is left as an API, which is used to integrate with the partner's inventory system. You should note that the number of blocks in the diagram doesn't necessarily reflect the number of code packages. For example, you can have all actor types defined in one code package; also, many web frameworks natively support packaging the frontend (HTML) together with the backend (APIs).

This is a fair first step. However, we need to think more about the booking process. As introduced in earlier chapters, booking a vacation package is a complex distributed transaction that may take minutes or even hours to complete. What we'll need is a way to drive multiple booking procedures in parallel. One way to achieve this is to use a Vacation Package actor to represent a package to be booked. The actor is given a desired state through the Traveler UI, and it uses a timer to check its state and tries to reconcile it with the desired state by calling the Inventory APIs of corresponding partners. We'll also bring in the separate job creation and processing design in Figure 6-4 so that we can decouple package generation and package booking. This is necessary in this case because package booking is a long process and we can't hold up user requests waiting for it. However, we won't use a messaging system in this case. Instead, the Traveler API simply launches new Vacation Package virtual actors when it receives a request.

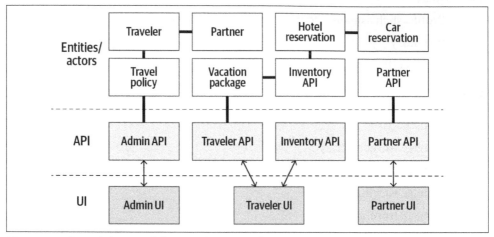

Figure 6-5. Initial design of the travel agent website

Figure 6-6 shows the updated architecture. In this updated design, the Traveler UI doesn't access the Inventory API anymore. Instead, calling the Inventory API becomes an implementation detail of the Vacation Package actor. The Traveler API directly accesses the actor state store to provide faster aggregations and flexible queries over existing bookings, and the Inventory API is updated to incorporate partner offers. Finally, all the relevant actor boxes have been updated to multiple boxes to indicate they can be horizontally scaled.

We think this is a decent design for a single tenant. For enterprise users, we have three options. The first is to deploy the entire stack per enterprise customer. The second is to make the administrative path multitenant. The third option is to make everything multitenant. The first option requires no code changes. However, it brings challenges when managing multiple customers, such as sharing partner inventory across deployments. The second option requires limited code changes, but you need to manage deployments for customers separately. This is not necessarily a bad thing, as different customers may have different scale factors and different policy update frequencies, and they may even want to use different hosting environments. Depending on your customer needs, having a separate stack per customer may turn out to be the best choice. The third option requires the most code changes, but it minimizes management overhead as you need to manage only a single global deployment.

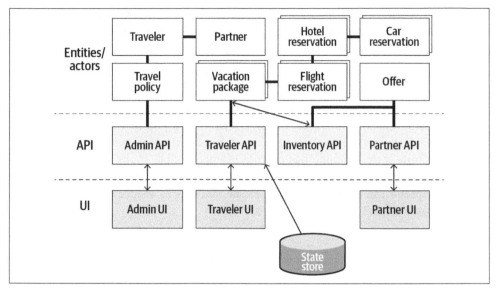

Figure 6-6. Updated travel agent website

Regardless of which route you choose, you should limit code customization to as few components as possible. In our scenario, it's most likely that the travel policies and the way the policies are reinforced will differ from user to user. To compensate for this, you may want to introduce a separate Policy Enforcer API to hide differences among users and to provide a standard API to the rest of the system.

A word of caution when you use such designs. If your actors do nothing more than encapsulate state and your APIs are not correctly segmented, you fall into the *blob* antipattern, in which a complex piece of code operates on many individual entities. In this particular scenario, you want the actors to be as autonomous as possible and the APIs to simply trigger activities on different actor instances.

So far, we've discussed how to take a legacy system and evolve it for the cloud, and how to design a moderately complex cloud native application from the ground up with Dapr. But an application rarely runs in isolation. It often needs to communicate with external systems. We'll discuss how you can use Dapr to integrate your application with external systems in the next section.

System Integrations with Dapr

We discussed a few message-based integration patterns in Chapter 3 when we introduced Dapr bindings. Message-based integration is an effective way to integrate multiple unrelated systems that are oblivious to each other. Indeed, there are various commercial products that serve this purpose, such as Microsoft BizTalk, Azure Logic Apps, and AWS Step Functions. You can certainly leverage community-contributed bindings or create your own custom bindings to connect to these systems, which are outside the scope of this book. The remainder of this section discusses a few more useful patterns for system integration using Dapr.

Distributed Workflow as Finite State Machine

When we discussed the Saga pattern in Chapter 3, we took an event-centric view—the workflow responds to various events and performs corresponding actions. A different approach to modeling the workflow is to treat it as a *finite state machine* (FSM). Simply put, a finite state machine has a finite list of possible states, and it transitions among the states based on inputs and its current state. For example, the sample workflow in Chapter 3 can be described by the state machine in Figure 6-7. For simplicity, it doesn't contain all the cancelation transitions.

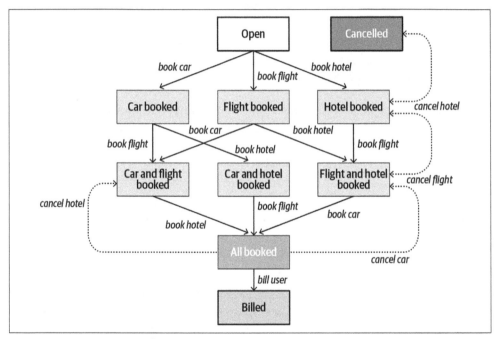

Figure 6-7. Booking workflow as FSM

You can easily model this state machine using a Dapr actor, which can expose the necessary methods to trigger the corresponding transitions. A key difference from the system in Chapter 3 is that the actor instance can decide whether a certain transition is allowed, compared to the workflow reconciling state with what already happened (expressed as events).

The FSM saves its state upon any successful state transition. This means an FSM can be shut down at any time and resume from its state as needed. In addition to requiring the state operations to be transactional, this design also requires the FSM to transit among only the defined states without using any intermediate states that might cause confusion when the FSM instance is relaunched.

A more detailed discussion of FSMs is out of the scope of this book, as a proper FSM implementation requires much more than what has been described here. We'll leave further exploration as an exercise for the reader. Next, we'll switch gears to focus on state synchronization for stateful applications.

Synchronization

A common task in system integration is to keep two or more systems in sync. Because the integrated systems are often coupled together by business processes, we need to make sure as the processes transit from one system to another that the data is in sync on both sides to avoid unnecessary conflicts. This section introduces a couple of patterns for the purpose.

Shared database

Having a shared database may sound like it introduces a tight coupling between two systems. However, for two remote systems with access to the same database, such as a cloud-hosted database, the shared database pattern provides an efficient way to synchronize large amounts of data between the systems. When implementing the pattern, you should consider setting up a database or a table specifically for the purpose of synchronization instead of forcing the systems to share the same database schema. This gives you more flexibility in evolving each system independently.

You can use Dapr to encapsulate state access. All you need to do is configure the two systems so that their state stores for synchronization are pointing at the same database location. If you want to implement a shared relational database, you'll need to write custom code and use Dapr to expose a synchronization API to the rest of your system. The benefit of using Dapr in this case is that you can also leverage Dapr's middleware mechanism to insert additional data handling features, such as normalization, batching, and compression, to further optimize data synchronization. Figure 6-8 illustrates a sample setup that uses Dapr to encapsulate a synchronization API and uses Dapr middleware to customize the data synchronization pipeline.

If a direct database share isn't feasible, you can leverage existing data synchronization solutions that support the database platforms of your choice. However, in such settings data is only eventually consistent, so you need to make sure the systems are designed to cope with temporary inconsistencies.

If you switch the shared database to a messaging backbone, the pattern transforms into the inbox/outbox pattern, which is introduced next.

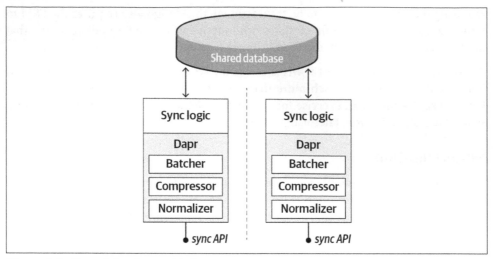

Figure 6-8. Shared database with Dapr

Inbox/outbox and mailman

Inbox/outbox is a simple and casual synchronization mechanism. Under this pattern, each system maintains an inbox and optionally an outbox. Whenever a system needs to sync with another system, it sends a message to the target system. The message contains the data to be synced, or instructions to get the updated data. This is not a rigid data synchronization pattern; instead, it allows systems to inform each other of changes. The recipients can choose to respond to these notifications or to discard them.

Relying on direct messaging among systems assumes that all systems know about each other—or that they at least know each other's inbox addresses. This is undesirable for two reasons: first, when a system needs to sync with multiple systems, it has to send a message to each of them; second, the inbox addresses have to be exchanged and configured on participating systems, which introduces management overhead. A different approach is to use pub/sub. Pub/sub allows a system to notify multiple systems at the same time, and it removes the need for a system to know the target inbox addresses. It simply publishes messages to an agreed topic. A caveat to this design is that because all systems subscribe to the same topic, a system needs to filter out the messages that it sends itself. An alternative design is for each system to publish to its own "outgoing" topic, to which the recipient systems subscribe. Figure 6-9 illustrates how three systems can keep in sync by sending messages to each other through (a) the inbox/outbox pattern, (b) pub/sub to a common topic, and (c) pub/sub through outgoing topics.

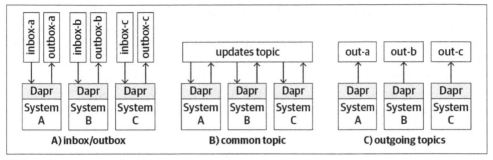

Figure 6-9. Variations of the inbox/outbox pattern

With the inbox/outbox pattern, you can also optionally bring in a *mailman*. The mailman is a centralized message handler that moves messages between inboxes and outboxes. The main benefit of using a mailman is that you can centrally manage integration topology and sync policies by controlling the mailman. You can also set up and scale a dedicated infrastructure to host the mailman to reduce the message processing burden on individual systems.

Synchronization through messaging is quite powerful, as it allows systems to be integrated but remain loosely coupled at the same time. Next, we'll examine a more disciplined pattern that can be used for synchronization through messaging.

Event sourcing

The gist of the event sourcing pattern is to treat all state mutations as events. For instance, when managing a bank account, instead of directly updating the account balance, all withdrawals and deposits are recorded as events. To get the account balance, you start with the initial balance, which is likely to be zero, and play back all the events that have ever occurred on the account. Of course, you'll want to implement some optimizations, such as periodically creating checkpoints of the balance and applying events only after the checkpoints.

There are many benefits and applications of the event sourcing pattern. First, you can return to any point in time in the system. This is quite powerful when you want to correct an earlier transaction. For example, if you want to correct a transaction that happened a month ago, you can rewind the system state to just before that transaction, apply the updated transaction, and then play back the rest of the recorded events. Second, the pattern allows you to ship the events to a different environment for diagnostic purposes. If you want to debug a problem that happened in the production environment, you can ship the events to a separate environment, play them back, and analyze the root cause of the problem. Then you can test out your solution on the copy of the production data and apply the change to production only when you are confident everything is in place. Third, the pattern uses append-only operations on the database. The idea is to avoid database updates, which are usually more expensive and less performant than insert operations. When you update a record, you need to place a lock on the record to avoid conflicting writes, and locks can lead to various problems such as lock escalation, deadlocks, and bottlenecks. The pattern can also separate updates from reads so that all read operations occur without interruptions from writes. The events can be played back and aggregated in different ways to generate repopulated views for fast queries. Finally, the pattern can be used to set up a backup and restore system. You can archive all the events and play them back to restore the system to any point in time.

You can use the event sourcing pattern for synchronization by shipping events from one system to another and playing them back in the other system. For example, in a master/secondary configuration, the master ships all its events to the secondary servers. When the master fails, a secondary server is elected the new master. Because synchronization between the master and the secondaries is usually done periodically in batches, however, you may lose the latest batch when the failover happens.

You can implement an append-only state store using Dapr's state store interface. Essentially, the `Set` method appends update events to the database instead of updating the existing records, and the `Read` method maintains checkpoints at a frequency based on the application's needs. It reads from the last known checkpoint and plays back the events from that point onward.

We've barely scratched the surface of system integration here. What we'd like to see is the Dapr community collectively building up best practices and patterns as well as tools and services for system integration.

Next, we'll provide a brief overview of how Dapr works with existing tools and frameworks to enable various scenarios. With the rapid development of Dapr, what we cover here will be just a small set of what's possible—but we hope we can provide a perspective on how Dapr can be helpful to different developer communities and empower them to achieve more.

Dapr in a Larger Ecosystem

Dapr has certainly attracted attention from many different communities. We are happy to see more and more teams enabling Dapr in their ecosystems and using it to build innovative solutions. This section offers a brief survey of some of the most interesting projects we've seen so far, starting with tooling.

Yeoman Dapr Generator

Yeoman (*https://yeoman.io*) is a popular scaffolding tool that can be used to scaffold many different types of applications. It's a great tool for developers to use to get up and running quickly when learning a new language or framework. Now there's a Yeoman Dapr generator (*https://oreil.ly/jhx5d*) that can help you to generate

Dapr-enabled applications in C#, Go, JavaScript, Python, and TypeScript. The generated code contains samples to use for method invocations and pub/sub, as well as bindings.

To use the generator, simply type yo dapr in a terminal window after you've installed Yeoman and the generator and follow the wizard to create a complete Dapr application.

Dapr in Visual Studio Code

Visual Studio Code is one of the most popular code editors in the world. Millions of developers use Visual Studio Code to work on their projects, in various programming languages and frameworks. As a language-agnostic runtime, Dapr fits nicely in this ecosystem. The Visual Studio Code team have seen the value of Dapr as well, so they've released a Dapr add-on (*https://oreil.ly/ufNb5*) in the Visual Studio Code Marketplace.

The best way to learn a tool is to try to use it (preferably with an experienced guide so you don't hurt yourself). So let's walk through a complete example of creating, running, and debugging a Dapr application using the Visual Studio Code extension.

The following steps are based on the preview release of the extension. The actual experience in the released version may differ.

To get started, follow these steps:

1. Install the Visual Studio Code Dapr add-on.
2. Create a new folder.
3. Open the folder in Visual Studio Code.
4. Press Ctrl-Shift-D to open the Run panel.
5. Click the "create a *launch.json* file" link to create a new launch configuration. Select Node.js as the target environment.
6. Close the generated *launch.json* file.
7. Press Ctrl-Shift-P to bring up the Command Palette.
8. Launch the Dapr: Scaffold Dapr Tasks command.
9. Select the default Launch Program configuration.
10. Enter nodeapp as the Dapr ID and press Enter to continue.
11. Leave the application port at the default of 3000 and press Enter to continue.

12. Create a Node.js application. You can reuse the Node.js greeting service from the Introduction.

13. In a Visual Studio terminal, run `npm install` to install the necessary Node.js packages.

14. Open the *app.js* file and set up a breakpoint at the `app.post` method.

15. Press Ctrl-Shift-D again.

16. In the Run panel, make sure you select the newly generated Launch Program with the Dapr launch profile, and then select the Run°Start Debugging menu item.

    You should observe that both your application and the Dapr sidecar are launched.

17. Press Ctrl-Shift-P to bring up the Command Palette.

18. Launch the Dapr: Invoke (POST) Application Method command.

19. Select `nodeapp` as the target app and `greeting` as the target method. Then enter a simple JSON payload, such as `{"a":"b"}`, and press Enter to send the request.

You should see that the breakpoint is hit, as shown in Figure 6-10.

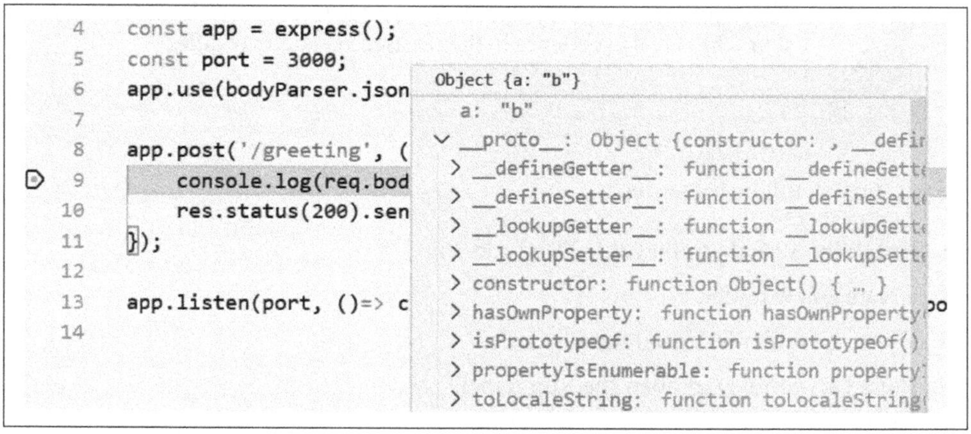

```
 4     const app = express();
 5     const port = 3000;
 6     app.use(bodyParser.json     Object {a: "b"}
 7                                   a: "b"
 8     app.post('/greeting', (   ∨ __proto__: Object {constructor: , __defir
⌖9          console.log(req.bod    > __defineGetter__: function __defineGette
10          res.status(200).sen    > __defineSetter__: function __defineSette
11     });                         > __lookupGetter__: function __lookupGette
12                                 > __lookupSetter__: function __lookupSette
13     app.listen(port, ()=> c     > constructor: function Object() { … }
14                                 > hasOwnProperty: function hasOwnProperty(00
                                    > isPrototypeOf: function isPrototypeOf()
                                    > propertyIsEnumerable: function property
                                    > toLocaleString: function toLocaleString
```

Figure 6-10. Debugging a Dapr application in Visual Studio Code

In addition to tooling support, we are also working with the community to provide deeper integration with existing frameworks, such as ASP.NET Core and Spring Boot. We'll look at an example of this next.

Dapr with ASP.NET Core

Dapr.AspNetCore (*https://oreil.ly/VOOxP*) is a NuGet package that allows you to easily integrate Dapr features such as state management and bindings into your ASP.NET Core web applications.

The NuGet package contains ASP.NET Core extensions that allow you to decorate your ASP.NET controllers to enable various Dapr functionalities. For example, the following code snippet (*https://oreil.ly/A2zTx*) demonstrates how you can make a controller stateful by accessing a value from the specified state store and key:

```
[HttpGet("{account}")]
public ActionResult<Account> Get([FromState(StoreName)]StateEntry<Account>
  account)
{
    if (account.Value is null)
    {
        return this.NotFound();
    }

    return account.Value;
}
```

And the following code snippet shows how you can bind a controller method to a messaging topic so that the method can be triggered not only by direct web requests but also by events published to the topic:

```
[Topic("deposit")]
[HttpPost("deposit")]
public async Task<ActionResult<Account>> Deposit(Transaction transaction,
      [FromServices] DaprClient daprClient) {
    var state = await daprClient.GetStateEntryAsync<Account>(StoreName,
          transaction.Id);
    state.Value ??= new Account() { Id = transaction.Id, };
    state.Value.Balance += transaction.Amount;
    await state.SaveAsync();
    return state.Value;
}
```

This is powerful. By "Daprizing" your ASP.NET Core controller, you are enabling the same API surface (and literally the same API code!) to be triggered by a messaging system. For example, the inbox/outbox pattern mentioned earlier in this chapter can easily be implemented through this annotation syntax. Without Dapr, you'd have to build up a messaging layer and figure out how to host that messaging layer together with your API layer. With Dapr, all you need to do is add the Topic annotation and configure your event source.

A Dapr sidecar is the companion of an individual microservice. A complex system usually consists of tens or even hundreds of microservices. In many cases, it's very desirable to be able to manage all these services as a single unit—an application. In the following section, we'll discuss how Dapr can be used in the context of a bigger application.

Dapr in a Bigger Application

At the time of writing, Dapr itself doesn't provide a way to describe a multicomponent application. This is because Dapr aims to be a programming model, not an application model. The difference between a programming model and an application model is that a programming model is concerned with how a processing unit or service is written, and an application model is concerned with the topology of the processing units.

As you've already learned, a Dapr sidecar can run as a process or a Docker container. Running as a standard container is great, because this means you can use any existing container tools and manifest formats to describe your workload together with the Dapr sidecar. For example, earlier in this book you saw a sample of how to enable a Dapr sidecar being injected into your application pod by adding Dapr annotations to your Kubernetes deployment pod specification:

```
annotations:
  dapr.io/enabled: "true"
  dapr.io/id: "nodeapp"
  dapr.io/port: "3000"
```

Similarly, you can describe Dapr sidecars in a Helm chart (*https://helm.sh*), package Dapr sidecars in a CNAB package (*https://cnab.io*), or deploy Dapr sidecars together with your applications using Knative (*https://knative.dev/*).

We've also talked about OAM (*https://oam.dev*), an open source project that aims to provide a developer-friendly modeling language that allows developers to design and describe their applications in a platform-agnostic fashion. Developers can design the exact logical topology of their applications, including components, their scale and connectivity, security scopes, and ingress routes. Then they can ship the application manifest to operations, who can realize these described intentions on specific platforms. For example, an operations team may choose to use Azure Load Balancer as the ingress when deploying the application to Azure and use a container-based Nginx proxy as the ingress when deploying the same application to an edge server. Such decisions can be made without developers' involvement, and the developers never need to be concerned with (or even know about) any infrastructural details.

OAM application models are managed by an OAM-compatible control plane. On Kubernetes, an OAM application model is usually composed of several customer resources managed by corresponding operators. Dapr works great with such control planes, as they often support Kubernetes pod annotations or similar mechanisms. See the documentation for your control plane of choice for more details on Dapr support.

Before we wrap up this part of the chapter, we'll address a common question.

Dapr and Service Meshes

We are often asked what the difference is between Dapr and existing service mesh solutions such as Istio, Linkerd, or Consul.

Dapr and service meshes do have some similarities. Because they both use the sidecar architecture, which was popularized by service meshes in the first place, many people's first reaction to Dapr is to wonder if this is another service mesh competitor. On the other hand, as Dapr evolves, it's starting to provide features that are more networking-related but are still application concerns, such as mutual TLS authentication.

The main difference between Dapr and service meshes is that they work at different levels. Service meshes manage the network traffic between services, so they work at an infrastructural level. Dapr, on the other hand, provides common building blocks such as state management to applications—so Dapr works at the application level. "Network mesh" probably would have been a better name for a service mesh, and then we could have called Dapr itself the service mesh. However, as the name "service mesh" is already taken, we sometimes refer to Dapr as an "application mesh" to distinguish it from service mesh technologies.

Because Dapr works at a different level and addresses a different set of concerns, Dapr sidecars work seamlessly with existing service mesh sidecars. If you configure them to work together, your application traffic will go through the Dapr sidecar first and then the service mesh sidecar, and it will go through the stack in the reverse order on the other end of the communication. Yes, there are multiple hops in this case, but that's a common price to pay for any type of abstraction.

At the time of writing, the Dapr team is working on a document that provides a more detailed comparison between Dapr and service meshes. Consult the online documentation for more details.

We'll close this chapter with a brief discussion of Dapr on edge, which we'll discuss more in Chapter 7.

Dapr on Edge

From day one, Dapr has been designed to be lightweight so that it works great on the edge. And we've been careful not to add any hard dependencies on Kubernetes or Docker containers so that Dapr can run outside Kubernetes in a containerless environment. Dapr is cross-compiled for major CPU architectures including x86_64, ARM64, and ARMv7, and people have succeeded in compiling Dapr into WebAssembly bytecode as well. So at a minimum, we can claim Dapr is edge-friendly.

And Dapr certainly works well on capable edge devices such as edge servers and Raspberry Pis.

The question, however, is whether Dapr is suitable for low-power devices with extremely limited capacity and strict power consumption constraints. At the time of writing, we think a fair answer is "it's unlikely." Dapr's sidecar architecture assumes the application is a web server, and Dapr itself runs as a web server as well. Even if we can ignore memory and CPU constraints, dealing with the power consumption of two web servers could be a challenge by itself.

One possible solution is to make Dapr into a library that can be loaded into the same workload process. In this case, the application leverages capabilities (such as messaging and state management) delivered by Dapr through native, in-process calls. And if the application doesn't expect inbound calls, it can be implemented as a regular process instead of a web server. Another possible solution is to keep the Dapr sidecar running on a more capable device, such as a field gateway. This design breaks the presumed security boundary between the application and the sidecar, however, and you'll have to consider how to support multiple devices through the same gateway.

The next chapter will present some ideas on how to extend Dapr further to support low-power devices in IoT scenarios.

Summary

Dapr is designed to support cloud native applications. It brings common functionalities to distributed applications through sidecars. Dapr is also designed for event-driven applications. It allows application code to respond to events from various event sources and to send events to other systems through connectors. Many distributed system, service-oriented design, and message-based integrated patterns work naturally with Dapr.

You can use Dapr to migrate legacy systems, or to develop new cloud native applications. Its unique, nonintrusive nature allows you to leverage Dapr to whatever extent you see fit. This means you can use Dapr together with other technologies, such as service meshes, without conflicts.

Thanks to contributions from our great community, Dapr is being integrated with many different platforms, frameworks, and toolchains, such as ASP.NET Core and Visual Studio Code. We are looking forward to seeing even more contributions from the community in the future. In the final chapter of the book, we'll take a peek to see what Dapr might become.

CHAPTER 7

Dapr's Future

 Disclaimer: The ideas in this chapter represent the personal opinions of the authors, based on discussions with some members of the community and of the Dapr team. They should not be interpreted as a roadmap of Dapr's future or planned features.

Dapr is still a young project. From its creation, it has aimed at being an open, vendor-neutral runtime that is helpful and nonintrusive. The future of Dapr will be shaped by the collective efforts of the entire Dapr community. Everyone is encouraged to join the community and to contribute new ideas and code.

As two of the first developers, the authors of this book have had the privilege to discuss Dapr's future with many different people coming from different perspectives. The goal of this chapter is to capture some of the ideas that have been shared, and hopefully to inspire new ideas and new application scenarios.

This chapter organizes the ideas about Dapr's future into several broad categories: capability delivery, actors, edge computing, and more. For each of the categories, it first presents the underlying rationales or trains of thought and then introduces some specific features inspired by these thoughts. In all cases, these are just a few examples of directions that Dapr is or may be heading in.

Capability Delivery

As you know by now, Dapr uses a sidecar architecture to deliver commonly required capabilities to distributed applications. This is best illustrated by the building block introductory diagram from the Dapr repository (*https://oreil.ly/_cTOx*), reproduced in Figure 7-1.

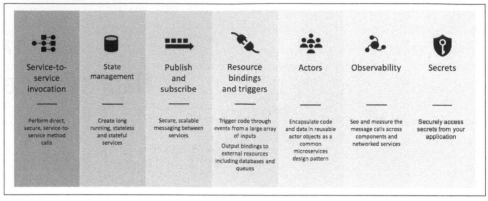

Figure 7-1. Dapr building blocks

As Dapr evolves, the number of building blocks increases. For example, the secrets building block was introduced only a few months before this book was written.

So far, it has been the core Dapr team that decides what building blocks to include in the Dapr runtime. However, it makes logical sense to enable additional building blocks to be introduced by the community. And it's also desirable to allow a customer to load only the set of building blocks they need, instead of always preloading all the blocks as is done in the current Dapr implementation.

To make Dapr a capability delivery vehicle we need only a few moderate extensions, which we'll discuss in the next section.

Architecture

When a Dapr sidecar launches, it reads and loads all configured components, such as state stores and message buses. Then it sets up a set of routes for each component, as shown in the following code snippet, which sets up state routes:

```
func (a *api) constructStateEndpoints() []Endpoint {
    return []Endpoint{
        {
            Methods: []string{http.Get},
            Route:   "state/<storeName>/<key>",
            Version: apiVersionV1,
            Handler: a.onGetState,
        },
        {
            Methods: []string{http.Post},
            Route:   "state/<storeName>",
            Version: apiVersionV1,
            Handler: a.onPostState,
        },
        {
            Methods: []string{http.Delete},
```

```
        Route:    "state/<storeName>/<key>",
        Version: apiVersionV1,
        Handler: a.onDeleteState,
    },
  }
}
```

We can use a similar mechanism to load capability packages. Although we can implement similar logic for new components to be loaded, we may consider automatically generating the routes by supporting some standard API descriptions, such as the OpenAPI Specification (*https://oreil.ly/DtEii*). Capability packages can either be loaded into the Dapr sidecar process as self-hosted packages or be configured to point to a remotely hosted API server, as shown in Figure 7-2. As shown in the figure, in the case of the remote API, a local API proxy (which can be autogenerated by OpenAPI tools) is configured to provide functional routes and to proxy requests to the remote server.

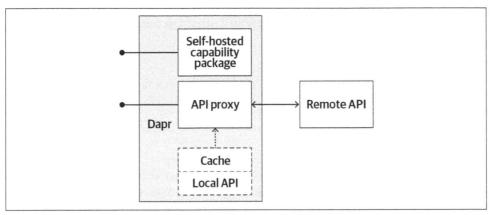

Figure 7-2. Dapr capability package

We can do more interesting things with the API proxy, too. For example, the proxy can maintain a local cache and serve repetitive requests directly from the cache, forwarding only the new requests to the remote server. This extra cache layer has several benefits:

- It provides better performance by serving cached results directly from the cache.
- It reduces the number of calls to the remote API. This reduces service consumption costs as well as avoiding possible throttling from the server.
- It helps to sustain system availability when the remote API becomes unavailable.

That's cool, but we can push even further. Imagine the capability package has associated metadata that looks something like this:

```
metadata:
  name: object-detection
  offers:
  - name: azure-cognitive-service
    type: OpenAPI
    reference: http://...
  - name: yolo
    type: Container
    reference: docker.io/some-image
```

As you can see, the manifest defines multiple offers of the same capability in different forms: remote API or local container. What the API proxy can do in this case is fall back to a local container instance when the remote API becomes unavailable. This is architecturally significant—the application can model its logic based on certain capabilities without needing to worry about where and how the capabilities are delivered, because everything is hidden behind Dapr routes.

When Dapr is extended as a generic delivery vehicle for arbitrary capabilities, it can support many interesting scenarios, which we'll briefly summarize next.

Application Scenarios

Using Dapr to bring capabilities to applications is not just a fancy way to service APIs. The architecture enables a few quite powerful scenarios. We'll explore some of them in this section.

Distributed API management

Many enterprises use various cloud services to support their own applications. It's often hard to keep track of all the service subscriptions or to reinforce policy controls over service consumption, especially when services from multiple cloud vendors are involved. Therefore, many enterprises use a centralized API management service that proxies all cloud service calls. Then they apply policies over the API management service to control service consumption.

Dapr offers a different approach to API management. With Dapr sidecars, the API proxies are distributed and colocated with the application code. This is a more scalable architecture compared to a centralized proxy. And because Dapr sidecars share configuration objects in the same cluster, you can still centrally manage your API policies by putting the policies into Dapr configurations. Furthermore, you can still gain a single pane of glass view of all API consumption by tapping into Dapr's distributed tracing capability.

When you combine the distributed API management capability with local caches and self-hosted capability alternatives, you have an efficient, scalable API management solution without any centralized pieces that can potentially become bottlenecks.

Compute push-out

One edge computing pattern is to push compute from the cloud out to the edge when appropriate. The pattern allows faster computation in context on edge devices. For example, Figure 7-3 shows a containerized web application being pushed out to telco edge sites or further down to on-premises datacenters, assuming a compatible hosting environment (such as Kubernetes) is available in all environments. Clients now have the option to connect to different hosting environments based on their latency, security, and data sovereignty policies, and Dapr's capability API can hide all the location and authentication differences. From the client's perspective, it always calls the web application through *localhost* without authentication, or through Dapr-provided TLS authentication.

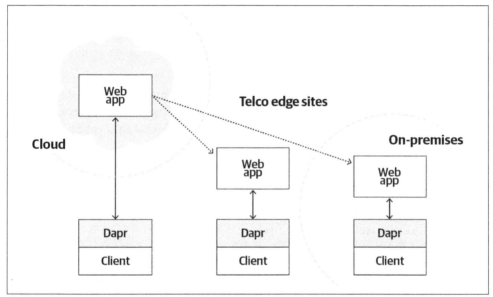

Figure 7-3. Compute push-out from cloud to edge

In a more advanced system, web application instances can be dynamically scaled to reduce the overall hosting cost while maintaining user satisfaction. For example, when lots of sports fans gather for a big football game, the team's web application instances can dynamically scale out on the telco edge site near the arena to handle the workload spike. During the off-season, all site deployments can be scaled down to zero and all clients directed to cloud-hosted instances for occasional accesses.

Also worth noticing is that with Dapr's capability delivery mechanism such compute push-out doesn't have to be centrally coordinated. If you update the earlier capability metadata to make it prefer the local container over remote API calls, the API proxy can pull down the latest image as needed and launch its own local copies. In other words, compute is *pulled down* to the edge instead being *pushed* from the cloud.

Artificial intelligence

Microsoft's AI strategy is making AI approachable for every developer and consumer. Dapr's capability API can wrap complex AI calls as simple, local API calls. For example, to detect objects in a picture, a developer can simply post the picture to a (fictional) URL:

http://localhost:3500/v1/capabilities/detect/object?as=rectangles

and Dapr will return tagged rectangles in the picture's coordinate system. The developer is concerned only with the object detection capability. It's up to the operations team to configure how the capability is delivered—as remote service calls, local containers, or in-process calls—and the API proxy can switch among different offerings as needed. For example, a smart traffic camera may rely on cloud-based AI modules for license plate recognition with high-resolution pictures when the connection allows. When the connection degrades, it may switch to an edge deployment with low-resolution pictures to ensure continuous service. Such changes remain transparent to the application developers.

Dapr's capability delivery mechanism enables application developers to design their applications using a capability-oriented architecture, a topic that deserves its own book. Next, we'll switch to the actor pattern and examine what innovations Dapr can bring to this popular programming model.

Enhanced Actors

As introduced in Chapter 4, Dapr supports a fully functional virtual actor pattern with native APIs as well as .NET and Java SDKs (and a Python SDK is actively being worked on at the time of writing). Dapr differs from other actor frameworks in an important way: it allows you to break out from the defined framework. This reflects a key principle of Dapr's design—be helpful, but not restrictive. Dapr is there to help, but when you are confident about going beyond Dapr, you are welcome to do so. This openness in architecture also allows us to provide some innovative actor features. The following sections introduce some of them.

Aggregators

Aggregating state from many actor instances can be problematic. Because an actor encapsulates its state, you can query an actor's state only through an access method it defines. This means that to aggregate state from multiple actors, you must probe them one by one and aggregate the results. The aggregated result is not a consistent snapshot of the overall system, because it's skewed by time differences between polls across actor instances. Even if you try to launch thousands of threads to poll all the connected devices in parallel, your snapshot will still be skewed because the threads are not synchronized.

Because Dapr doesn't use a proprietary actor state format, you can easily query actor states by going directly to the underlying data store. Furthermore, you can use the database's native transaction isolation to achieve desired isolation levels such as *read uncommitted* and *serializable*. By querying the database directly, you can take a consistent snapshot of all actor states with the cost of a single database query.

An aggregator actor encapsulates such queries into an easily consumable interface that can perform common aggregations such as sum(), average(percentile p), and histogram (bands b).

Query Interface

We can push the aggregator idea further to allow more flexible queries. The aggregator actor can define an open query interface that allows the user to run queries written in standard formats such as oData, T-SQL, and Gremlin.

Of course, we need to place constraints to disallow running arbitrary and potentially dangerous queries, such as deleting the database table. This can be done by configuring the actor state store with appropriate RBAC settings that grant designated users read-only access to specific database entities.

If allowing arbitrary queries is considered too dangerous, we can instead enable grouping and filtering of actors by metadata. For example, if we allow actor instances to be associated with tags, we can offer a limited query capability that supports filtering by tags. To query all elevator cars (represented by actors) that are due for maintenance, a user could run a query that filters elevators by last recorded maintenance date.

Next, we'll extend the aggregated actor idea, which defines a one-to-many mapping, to support generic graph topologies.

Actor Graph

An actor graph allows multiple actor instances to be dynamically linked together into a graph that can be treated as a single actor instance. For example, suppose you have two actor instances, instance A and instance B. You can link them together by attaching instance B as a dependent of instance A. Once they are linked, you can't update any of the instances anymore. However, you'll be able to operate on the combined instance as a new actor instance. The new instance follows the general operational principles, such as a single-threaded access pattern and transactional state update. The combined actor instance exposes the same interface as the individual actor instances, and when it receives a call it dispatches the call to individual actor instances by following the dependency links.

Let's consider a specific scenario in order to better explain possible applications of an actor graph. Imagine you've modeled different parts of a vehicle as individual actors.

They work together by calling each other or by exchanging messages through a message bus. Now you want to push a configuration update to some or all of the parts. The configuration update should be transactional, which means it should either be applied to all the affected parts at the same time or not be applied at all. What you will be able to do is join all the affected actors into a single graph and send the new configuration to the graph instance. The graph instance ensures all configuration updates are either committed or rolled back, and then you can release the parts from the graph.

Aggregators, actor graphs, and query interfaces allow you to access information across multiple actor instances simultaneously—a capability that is required by many IoT scenarios but frequently absent in actor frameworks.

Now let's turn our attention to individual actor instances and see what kinds of improvements we can make.

Multiversion Actors

In many IoT scenarios, we'd like to keep a brief history of actor state. For example, instead of reading just the latest reading from a sensor, we can get smoother readings by reading a moving average over a small window. A multiversion actor automatically maintains the last n versions of the actor state. In addition to regular state access methods, it also supports methods such as `moving_average`, `max`, `min`, and `median`.

Multiversion actors can also be configured to trigger actions based on how the state changes over the history window. For example, an acoustic sensor can be configured to respond to sudden changes in readings (by calculating the derivative of amplitude changes, for example) to detect pulsive sounds such as gunshots. Such a capability can be used to simplify signal detection and abnormality detection, making it much easier to implement certain IoT scenarios. For example, when multiple acoustic sensors are triggered, you can leverage the query interface to find activated sensors. Then you can use their geographic locations as well as signal time to calculate the exact location of the sound source (the shooter) by triangulation based on time difference of arrival (TDoA). Figure 7-4 illustrates how four sensors (A, B, C, and D) can collaborate to detect a gunshot location (S) in a 2D space. Each pair of sensors can generate a hyperbola based on TDoA; the common intersection of the hyperbolas decides where the gunshot originated.

Because we access Dapr actor instances through the Dapr sidecar, we can dynamically extend or modify actors using Dapr middleware, which we will briefly discuss next.

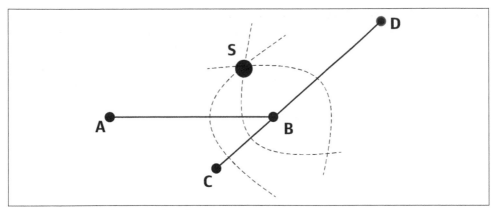

Figure 7-4. Example of gunshot detection

Actor Middleware

Just as we can use middleware to modify the Dapr sidecar's behavior, we can use middleware on top of actor state access methods. We can plug in various data transformation or normalization middleware to enable data interoperability without modifying the actors themselves. The middleware can also be designed to support multiple transformations. For example, it can be designed to project the same actor state to different shapes so that it can be consumed by consumers that expect different data formats, or different versions of the data format.

As you can see, Dapr actors are more easily extensible than those in some other actor frameworks—and the ideas presented here are just a few examples of directions we can go in. As mentioned earlier in this book, we believe a framework should provide developers with a golden path to success but allow them to explore and grow at the same time. Of course, this places higher expectations on the developers, but we think encouraging growth and innovation is a healthy thing to do for the sake of the whole industry.

Next, we'll move on to yet another fascinating topic: cross-cluster communications.

The Universal Namespace

Dapr sidecars can communicate with each other when they are on the same Kubernetes cluster. This is because for each sidecar Dapr automatically creates a `ClusterIP` service, whose address can be resolved by the built-in Kubernetes name resolution mechanism within the scope of the same cluster.

If a Dapr sidecar on one cluster wants to communicate with another Dapr sidecar on a different cluster, you can either use messaging (through a shared message bus) or expose the target sidecar by assigning it a public IP address.

The idea of the universal namespace is to allow Dapr sidecars to discover and communicate with each other using extended Dapr IDs with cluster postfixes. For example, a Dapr sidecar with ID `dapr-a` running on a cluster named `cluster-a` can address a `dapr-b` sidecar running on `cluster-b` by the name `dapr-b.cluster-b`. If you have a hybrid solution that spans across a cloud-based cluster and an edge-based cluster, the services running on either cluster can then talk to each other through universal namespace as if they were on the same cluster.

There are many potential ways to implement universal namespaces. The following section introduces one of the possible architectures.

Architecture

The most straightforward way to design a universal namespace solution is to use a reverse proxy that takes requests from a foreign cluster and forwards the requests to the appropriate services. The reverse proxy addresses, together with the site names they represent, can be cross-entered to all participating clusters, or the proxy addresses can be entered as DNS entries that are shared between clusters.

Figure 7-5 illustrates a possible implementation of a universal namespace with reverse proxies. In this setting we have two sites, `site_a` and `site_b`, which are interconnected through a private peered network. `site_a` hosts a service named `service_a` and `site_b` hosts two services, `service_b` and `service_c`. In a shared DNS table, remote names with site postfixes are pointed to the corresponding proxy addresses. When a service calls a local service (such as `service_b` calling `service_c`), because `service_c` resolves to the local cluster IP (which is routable only within the cluster), the call goes directly to the other service. When a service calls a remote service, the call is forwarded to the reverse proxy on the target cluster through an IP that is routable across clusters. The reverse proxy forwards the request to the target service (by stripping the site name off the address) and sends the result back to the caller.

If a service exposes a publicly routable IP by itself, the DNS records can be modified so that the remote service name resolves directly to the routable IP instead of going through the reverse proxy.

The architecture works when the clusters are connected over the internet. In this case, the reverse proxies need to be associated with public IP addresses. Because Dapr supports mutual TLS, it can automatically set up mutual TLS between the proxies. Furthermore, because all cross-cluster traffic goes through the reverse proxies (except for the publicly exposed services), you can easily set up the necessary network policies on the reverse proxies to protect the cross-cluster communication.

Another possible solution is to leave cross-cluster routing to a service mesh such as Linkerd, but we won't discuss that further here.

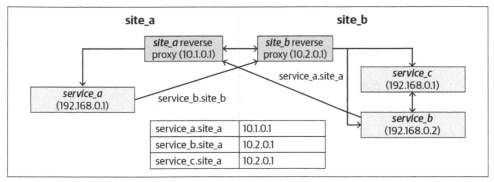

Figure 7-5. Universal namespace with reverse proxies

Application Scenarios

Universal namespaces allow services across multiple clusters to communicate with each other. In many enterprise environments, you may want to intentionally distribute your application components across clusters. For example, you may want to deploy your business logic components into a demilitarized zone (DMZ) that is separate from your frontend components residing on a public-facing network. The universal namespace allows Dapr sidecars running on different network segments to communicate with each other.

This capability is also very useful when you have services distributed across multiple clusters, such as at geographically separated sites. Figure 7-6 shows an example of accessing a geo-redundant service through the universal namespace. In this scenario, service_b is deployed at two physically separate sites, site_b and site_c. At site_a, the DNS table or routing table is configured with a remote service name (ser vice_b.other in the diagram) associated with both reverse proxies at the target sites. When service_a tries to invoke service_b.other, the traffic is split among the two proxies. When a site becomes unavailable, the routing table can be updated so that all traffic is routed to the remaining site.

The universal namespace can also be helpful in some cloud–edge hybrid scenarios. For example, a field gateway host can be a multinode Kubernetes cluster that runs the gateway service as a highly available service. The gateway service can use the universal namespace to maintain two-way communication with cloud-side services.

Next, we will take a look at what Dapr can do in edge computing scenarios, which we briefly introduced in Chapter 6.

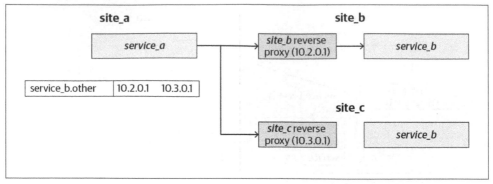

Figure 7-6. Accessing a geo-redundant service through the universal namespace

Dapr on Edge

Dapr is designed for both the cloud and the edge. However, so far its primary focus has been on enabling cloud native applications. We still have a long way to go to make Dapr a powerful runtime for the edge as well. This section covers a few topics that demonstrate different ways that Dapr can bring value to edge computing scenarios.

Dapr as a Lightweight Function Runtime

A function is a piece of code that can be triggered by an event. It takes some inputs, applies some calculations, and generates some outputs. Dapr possesses all the necessary basic features to be used as a function runtime. It supports triggers that can be used to activate function code, and it supports bindings that the function code can use to send data to another system. Dapr also has a few other features that make it a nice function runtime:

Stateful function support
 A function is generally stateless—it applies some transformation on the input and goes out of the picture. However, stateful functions can come in handy in some scenarios. For example, when you need to trigger an activity that depends on completion of a group of other activities, you can design the activity as a stateful function. When a prerequisite function finishes, it reports to the stateful function. The stateful function tracks all prerequisites and triggers its own logic when all prerequisites are met.

Language neutral
 Many function frameworks support only a limited selection of programming languages. Dapr supports all modern languages. This means you can write your function code in the language of your choice.

Simple runtime stack

The Dapr runtime runs as a single process. Although it's complemented by other Dapr services, such as the placement service, the Dapr runtime itself is enough to support common function executions. This makes it straightforward to package and distribute the runtime for edge deployments.

To use the Dapr runtime as a function runtime, your function code needs to be implemented as an HTTP or gRPC server. It is reasonable to expect that Dapr will be extended in the future to dynamically load the function code so that you don't have to host that code yourself.

One possible way to implement this is to use a process manager. Basically, you implement and package your function code as an executable or a batch/shell script and then you register with the process manager to inform it how to launch your executable with input parameter switches. The following code snippet shows a sample registration model that registers a *hello-world.sh* script with the process manager:

```
registration:
  name: hello-world
  cmd: ~/scripts/hello-world.sh
  input-switch: input
  id-switch: id
  input-type: inline
  runtime: bash
```

The process manager in turn registers `hello-world` as a function route with the Dapr runtime (acting as a function runtime). When the function is triggered, the Dapr runtime invokes the function code by calling the designated script with an `--input` switch and an `--id` switch:

```
~/scripts/hello-world.sh --id <function id> --input <function input>
```

You may have noticed the `runtime` property in the registration. The idea is that you can choose from a few supported runtimes, such as Docker and WebAssembly, to run your function code in a sandboxed environment, assuming your function code is already packaged for the runtime.

The process manager can be used to enable legacy applications to work as functions. For example, you can write a script that launches a legacy UI-based application and then send function input to the UI handle by sending keystrokes and copying data through the clipboard. Then you can register the script as a function with Dapr.

Having a lightweight function runtime available on the edge is a great extension to a Function-as-a-Service (FaaS) platform. The same cloud-based function can be pulled down to edge machines for faster response times and for disconnected scenarios. There are different means available to pull down function packages to the client, such as through a Docker registry. The most interesting option is to use the WebAssembly runtime; we'll look at that next.

Dapr in WebAssembly

WebAssembly (or *Wasm* for short) has been causally mentioned a couple of times in earlier chapters. In case you are not familiar with it, WebAssembly is an instruction format for a stack-based virtual machine. For example, the following is a simple WebAssembly module that exposes an add function that adds two integers together (the code is written in text format instead of binary format for better readability):

```
(module
  (func (param $a i32) (param $b i32) (result i32)
local.get $a
local.get $b
i32.add))
```

There is nothing really that interesting about the language itself—what's more interesting is the runtime that supports the language. Specifically, because the runtime is a World Wide Web Consortium (W3C) recommendation, it's supported by major modern browsers such as Google Chrome and Microsoft Edge. That gives it a tremendous reach: it's a pervasive runtime that provides a sandboxed execution environment in literally billions of computers around the world.

We're all familiar with content delivery networks (CDNs), which serve static content from distributed proxy servers instead of from the original servers. A CDN provides great acceleration in the user experience, and it allows a website to serve many more customers beyond the original server's capacity. With WebAssembly we can push more complex computation to the browser, enabling us to deliver smooth and sophisticated user interactions—such as gaming and online editing—right in the browser.

In theory, you can package your web server logic as WebAssembly and ship it to user browsers. This means you can deliver highly interactive websites with local performance to your end users, while all your web server does is serve static web pages and WebAssembly modules (both of which can be cached in the CDN).

Taking this idea further, if you can get Dapr to work as a WebAssembly module, your web pages will be able to use the module to consume all capabilities delivered by Dapr, such as saving state and connecting to various cloud services. Figure 7-7 shows an example of a web server running on a user's browser as a WebAssembly module behind a Dapr sidecar. The diagram shows how multiple browsers run their own local instances of the web server and use Dapr to share state and to communicate with the messaging backbone. The diagram also shows how when the capability delivery idea is combined into this design the Dapr sidecar can acquire additional capability packages, which are packaged as WebAssembly modules in this case, to enhance the web server's capabilities.

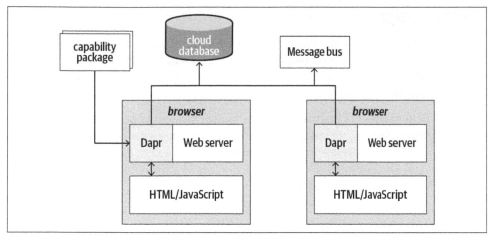

Figure 7-7. Web server as a WebAssembly module running in the browser

This design can also be used in crowdsourcing solutions. One of the key challenges of crowdsourcing is convincing your potential users to install your local calculation package. With this design, all the user needs to do is give their consent to run your calculation package; they can then dynamically acquire and run the package directly in their browser and use Dapr to send the calculation results back to your server. We can imagine there being a common website that allows users to browse and contribute to various crowdsourcing projects with just a few clicks.

Internet carriers could also get very creative with the internet connectivity devices in users' homes by running Dapr on these devices. For example, if you agreed to contribute the extra compute power in your modem or TV set-top box, you could earn credits by allowing your carrier to run sandboxed web servers on your devices. This agreement would allow the internet carriers to host web services using distributed devices. When carefully chosen, these devices can offer better latency and throughput to the target users without requiring complex infrastructure. Developments like this could usher in a new era of "edge cloud," which could be a real challenge to the traditional cloud platforms.

At the time of writing, more and more out-of-browser WebAssembly runtimes are emerging. These lightweight runtimes, which are sometimes just a few tens of kilobytes in size, are designed for low-power devices. And if we include some common interfaces such as the Open Container Initiative (OCI), Container Runtime Interface (CRI), or even `kubelet` on top of WebAssembly, these low-power devices can be joined to a Kubernetes cluster and have work scheduled on to them. This allows you to form a highly available hosting environment out of low-power devices.

Next, we'll continue with our thoughts on low-power devices and see how Dapr can be adapted for such environments.

Dapr as a Script

As discussed in the previous chapter, running a Dapr sidecar on a low-power device might be too expensive. One possible solution is to run the Dapr sidecar on a field gateway and have the devices communicate with the sidecar through a predefined IP address instead of *localhost*.

What if a field gateway is unavailable? In this case Dapr could be packaged as a script that low-power devices can call to invoke it. The reason for using script instead of a library is that it's more in keeping with Dapr's language-agnostic nature and dynamic composability. For example, when the device wants to save state, it can run the Dapr script with necessary command-line parameters:

```
dapr.sh --capability state --action save --key my-key --value "Hello, World!"
--store my-store
```

The Dapr CLI already has some built-in features to invoke the Dapr runtime, such as publishing a message to a topic. If it's extended to self-host a Dapr runtime, it can be used as a fully functional Dapr script.

The main benefit of running Dapr as a script is to avoid keeping a Dapr sidecar running, which may add power consumption pressure. However, repeatedly launching the Dapr runtime can be expensive for a low-power device as well. If this becomes a concern, implementing Dapr as a library could be a way out—this would bind you to specific programming languages but preserve all the meaningful abstractions and the dynamic configurability of Dapr. Thus, implementing the Dapr runtime as an in-proc library in popular edge computing languages such as Python, C++, and Rust could be a good addition to the Dapr ecosystem on the edge. Such efforts will also help enforce separation between the Dapr runtime and communication protocol, enabling integration with device communication protocols such as the Data Distribution Service (DDS) wire protocol.

As you can see, there are multiple paths Dapr can take to make its way to the edge—and we are certain the community will come up with yet more creative ways. Edge computing will be the center of computer science in the next 10 years. It will be great if Dapr can be part of the movement.

In the last section of this chapter, we will move on to discuss a few ideas for improvements that are harder to precisely categorize. Again, this is just a selection of examples of developments that have been suggested or that may be on the horizon.

Other Dapr Improvements

We have discussed many ideas about Dapr's future within the Dapr core team. This section captures some of the ideas that have come up in past discussions but have not made it onto the roadmap yet. Obviously, the situation may have changed by the time you're reading this text; we invite you to consult the latest online Dapr docs for updated information. The following topics are not sorted in any way.

Dapr Component Projection

Dapr components are described as YAML files, and when running on Kubernetes they are represented as Kubernetes custom resources. These components capture external dependencies of your application, such as a managed database or a load balancer. However, Dapr doesn't provide a built-in way to manage these external dependencies as a complete technical stack that your application relies on. Wouldn't it be nice if there were a way to easily describe and manage the dependencies to ensure that your application is well supported?

If you're thinking, "Wait a minute, that's a solved problem," you're right. Cloud platforms already offer resource management systems, such as Azure Resource Manager (ARM) and AWS CloudFormation, and there are cross-platform solutions such as HashiCorp's Terraform. These systems provide you with description languages you can use to describe the desired states of your cloud resources, and they try to bring all the required resources to the desired states. When any resource deviates from the desired state, the system can take corrective actions so that the resource is brought back to that state.

If Dapr doesn't want to reinvent any wheels, shouldn't we just use one of the existing solutions? The answer is yes! We certainly do not want to solve the resource management problem again. However, we're still missing a piece of the puzzle—how to project the cloud resources into Kubernetes custom resources. If there is automatic projection, we do not need to manually define Dapr components anymore. That is, we don't have to look up how to describe a Dapr component; instead, we can use any available resource management solution and have selected resources automatically projected into Kubernetes as Dapr components.

There are few benefits to this solution:

No manual component configuration
    This reduces the burden of managing a Dapr-based system.

Extensibility
    Once the projection is in place, any cloud resources can be projected into Dapr as components.

Automatic component configuration updates

> The projection system can be hooked up to underlying resource management systems and automatically update component definitions as needed when the original cloud resources change (such as when a key rotation occurs). This again reduces the management burden and the risk of bugs caused by infrastructure configuration mismatches.

Implementing such a projection system isn't hard, because these cloud resources have well-defined manifest schemas and API interfaces. It's theoretically feasible to auto-generate Dapr component code so that you don't need to write any custom code. Of course, a straight passthrough of resource APIs introduces little extra value. Dapr can still define a common API for certain resource types. Because the API will be a subset of the resource features, this part can also be captured as some sort of manifest and be generated automatically.

Best Practices and Proven Patterns

Dapr has implemented some best practices in its components, such as automatic retries upon transient errors with exponential backoff, configurable concurrency control, built-in secret management, and mutual TLS support. And as you've seen, you can use Dapr to easily implement some enterprise patterns, such as competing consumers and distributed workflows.

However, Dapr can do more. Dapr is well positioned to bring even more proven patterns and best practices to applications in a natural, friction-free way. For example, we can extend the retry pattern to support automatic circuit breaking. When a remote service is broken, it is pointless to keep trying it after a few attempts. Instead, a circuit breaker can be tripped, causing any future calls to fail without any attempt being made to contact the server until a configured time window has passed (at which point the circuit breaker is reset).

Another interesting pattern to support is event sourcing, discussed in Chapter 6. Event sourcing is a powerful pattern, but a proper implementation is hard to come by. The hope is that Dapr can eventually provide a solid event sourcing implementation, drawing on the power of its awesome community.

An interesting thing about Dapr is that it allows some of these patterns to be introduced and reconfigured independently from the application code. If you leverage a common patterns and practices library, the application code may misuse the library, causing inconsistent or unexpected behavior. When the patterns are applied through the Dapr sidecar, the rigidness in the usage pattern ensures consistency, and you have visibility into how these patterns are configured and applied. Being able to reinforce best practices without modifying the code is quite powerful. As a company's policies change, perhaps because of compliance requirement changes, the operations team can reconfigure the applications to make them compliant without touching the code.

Dapr Descriptor

The Dapr sidecar defines a simple and clear API for clients. It also defines a clear API to interact with application code. This means that you can describe the API shape of your application as well as its required components in a single descriptor file, and you can use an autogeneration tool to scaffold the skeleton of your application, along with its *Dockerfile*, deployment artifacts, and build scripts. Then you can insert your business logic into the generated HTTP handlers. The following code snippet shows what such a descriptor might look like:

```
services:
- name: my-service
  routes:
   - say-hello
   - say-goodbye
components:
- name: my-store
  type: state.redis
  metadata:
   - name: redisHost
     value: <Redis host>
   - name: redisPassword
     Value: <Redis password>
```

Some independent software vendors create applications in large numbers. These applications follow a similar design and structure but are designed for specific customers. Using a descriptor like this allows them to create these applications with great consistency without needing to repeat boilerplate code. Scaffolding is an alternative to shared libraries. They both aim at ensuring consistency across projects. However, designing and maintaining an efficient shared library is not an easy task, because the library must be reusable yet remain customizable to fit into different projects. Scaffolded code does not rely on a shared library, so it has more flexibility to be deeply customized for a specific project.

Dapr to Facilitate Multiparty Computing

The Dapr sidecar can be used to encapsulate complex multiparty computing protocols such as blockchain smart contracts and various gossip protocols. For the blockchain case, developers will be able to invoke a smart contract through a simple Dapr POST, or to configure the smart contract to be automatically triggered by any supported event sources. This brings blockchain to the broader developer community without friction.

Summary

As we've mentioned, Dapr is a young project. We are glad to have brought it to where it is today, and we are eager to see how Dapr will grow in the future. Whatever directions it goes in, we hope it will remain a helpful, humble, efficient runtime that empowers developers to write scalable and reliable distributed applications for both cloud and edge computing.

This chapter covered a small sample of ideas on how Dapr might evolve. We hope it has provided you with some inspiration, and we look forward to seeing what other ideas the community will come up with—come join us!

Index

Apache Cassandra state store, 47, 50
  Cassandra Query Language, 50
API
  Dapr API
    about, 21
    independent from delivery protocols, 17
    invoking Dapr actor, 103
    runtime implementing, 21
  Dapr state API
    about, 42
    bulk operations and transactions, 41
    data handling, 46
    data hashes instead of sets, 47
    data querying and aggregation, 46
    Delete requests, 44, 53
    Get requests, 43, 53
    implementing, 52
    Init method, 53
    key scheme, 43
    Multi method, 54
    REST API POST request, 17
    Set requests, 43, 53
    Transactional requests, 44
    working with, 45-47
  descriptor file, 153
  designing a cloud native application,
    120-123
  distributed API management, 138
  interface explicitly defined as, 115
  OpenAPI specifications, 137
  Policy Enforcer API, 123
  secret API, 89
applications
  cloud native applications, 4, 111
  consistently deployed, 112
  Dapr as programming model, 132
  Dapr sidecars integrated with, 132
  descriptor file, 153
  designing a cloud native application,
    120-123
  future of Dapr, 138
  loose coupling, 13
    (see also loose coupling)
  monolithic evolving to cloud, 116-119, 147
  MTTR of, 112
  Open Application Model, ix, 31
    application configuration, 32
  platform agnosticism importance, 33
  scaffolding tool Dapr generator, 128

security necessary, 79
  (see also security)
singleton characteristics, 117
universal namespace scenarios, 145
architecture
  about, 20-22
  Capability Oriented Architecture, 75
  component flexibility from, 113
  designing a cloud native application,
    120-123
  future of Dapr, 136
  microservice isolation of services, 57
  universal namespace, 144
artificial intelligence via Dapr, 140
ASP .NET (see .NET)
authentication
  access control, 80
  Active Directory, 116
  authorization versus, 80
  Azure Active Directory, 80
  monolithic application evolution, 119
  secret API not requiring, 89
authorization
  access control, 80
  authentication versus, 80
  OAuth 2.0 authorization, 22
availability
  cloud native application design, 114
  cloud promise and challenge, 2
  message-based integration and, 14
  stateful services, 38
  stateless services, 37
AWS DynamoDB state store, 47
Azure
  Azure Active Directory, 80
    updating to, 117
  Azure Container Instances, 6
  Azure Kubernetes Service, 8
  Cosmos DB
    about, 48
    available state stores, 47
    consistent read, 43
  Event Hub binding, 44
    metrics in Portal, 45
  Monitor
    exporters for, 26
    tracing with, 28

B

backend state store read-only access, 47
begin working with Dapr (see getting started)
best practices and proven patterns, 152
bindings
    about, 22, 42, 59
    autoscaling with KEDA, 69
    Azure Event Hub binding, 44
    Dapr input bindings, 64-66
        implementing, 66
    Dapr output bindings, 64, 66
        implementing, 68
    dynamic binding, 18
    Kubernetes mode, 46
    standalone mode, 43-45
    web service triggered by cloud events, 20
blob antipattern, 123
blob events triggering web services, 20
browser/server (B/S) architecture, 2
bulk operations and transactions
    Dapr state management, 41
        BulkDelete method, 53
        BulkSet method, 44, 53
    Lua script for Set and Delete requests, 47
busybox pod, 8

C

C#
    Dapr actor under .NET, 107-109
    Hello World via gRPC, 36
caching stateless services, 37
cancelations of distributed transactions, 73
Capability Oriented Architecture (COA), 75
Carr, Kathleen, x
Cassandra state store, 47, 50
    Cassandra Query Language, 50
Certificate Authority (CA)
    about certificates, 90
    identified by certificate, 91
    Sentry, 21, 92
certificate signing request (CSR), 92
certificate stores, 91
    Trusted Root Certificate Authorities store,
        91
certificates
    Certificate Authority certificates, 91
    X.509 certificates, 90
        requesting, 92
child spans, 25

claims from tokens, 80
CLI (command line interface)
    about, 20
    about Dapr, 20
    Dapr as script, 150
    Docker required, 23
    Hello World, standalone mode, 25
    installing, 23
    pub/sub, 62
    switches
        dapr run, 25
        init kubernetes, 30
    version, 24
client spans, 25
client/server (C/S) architecture, 2
cloud
    actors, 103
    application security, 80
    challenges of, 2
    cloud native applications
        about, 4, 111
        cloud environment, 112
        Dapr designed for, 31, 116
        deployment consistency, 112
        design of, 114
        designing, 120-123
        monolithic application evolution,
          116-119
        Open Application Model, 31
    cloud versus on-premises, 112
        errors embraced, 112
        horizontal scale, 113
    CloudEvents spec, 16, 60
    component projection, 151
    events triggering web services, 20
    failure of servers, 37
    infrastructure
        about, 5
        containers, 5
        IaaS, 6
        PaaS, 6
        SaaS, 6
    push compute to edge, 139
        pull down to edge, 139
    service invocation, 6
    shared database for synchronization, 125
    stateless service preference, 2, 4, 36
Cloud Native Computing Foundation (CNCF),
    16

Daprizing code snippet, 131
network security via access control, 82
New instance of state store, 54
Node.js message listener, 30-35
NuGet Dapr .NET core, 131

O

OAM (see Open Application Model)
OAuth 2.0 authorization, 22
online resources (see resources)
Open Application Model (OAM)
    about, 31, 132
    application as services interconnected, ix, 31
    Dapr designed for, 30, 31, 33
    OpenAPI specifications, 137
    traits, 32
        (see also components)
Open Enclave SDK, 84
open source, x, 18
OpenAPI specifications, 137
OpenCensus exporters, 26
OpenTelemetry for tracing
    about, 22, 25
    OpenCensus exporters, 26
Operations method of output bindings, 69
operator component, 21
optimistic concurrency, 17, 41
Orleans virtual actors framework, 96
output bindings, 59
    Dapr bindings, 64, 66
        implementing, 68

P

PaaS (Platform as a Service), 6
    monolithic code evolution, 116
parent spans, 25
partitioning for scaling out, 3, 39
    multiple state stores, 46
    partition ID, 39
    resource balancing, 39
    static versus dynamic, 39
performance and message-based integration, 14
phishing attacks, 91
PHP
    creating PHP service, 10
    deploying the service, 11
    exposing -dapr service, 12
pipelines
    custom, 19

event bindings, 59
    Kubernetes-based Event Driven Autoscaling, 70
pipelines for messages, 58
placement service
    about, 21, 99
    Docker required, 23
    explained, 100-103
platform agnosticism
    about Open Application Model, 31
    actors and callers, 99, 103
    bindings for, 42
    containerized and noncontainerized, 5
    Dapr designed for, 30, 31, 33
    importance of, 33
    infrastructure isolation of cloud native
        applications, 115
Platform as a Service (PaaS), 6
    monolithic code evolution, 116
Policy Enforcer API, 123
ports
    Hello World
        Kubernetes, 35
        standalone, 25
    invoking a Dapr actor, 103
    required, 23
    service invocation, 7, 9
POST request to save state, 17
power-constrained devices and Dapr, 134
    Dapr as script, 150
PowerShell script for pub/sub, 61
primary replication server, 38
programming model unified, 19
pub/sub
    about, 15
    custom component registration, 55
    Dapr pub/sub
        about, 15
        behaviors, 63
        extending, 63
        interface, 63
        PowerShell script, 61
        testing with CLI, 62
    events are published, 58
    example with subs and GUI pub, 63
    listening for events, 61
    message-based integration, 13
    messaging backbone, 16
    publishing an event, 61

synchronization via, 126
public key infrastructure (PKI) standard, 90
pulling messages, 58
pushing messages, 58
Python
    actor support, 99
    message sending, 30-35

Q

query interface, 141

R

rate limiting for security, 85
reactive programming, 58
Reaktive, ix
    (see also Dapr)
recovery point objective, 38
Redis
    init configuring, 27, 52
    messaging
        consumer groups, 61
        init configuring, 27, 52
        Streams as backbone, 22, 16, 61
        Streams described, 61
    state store
        about, 47
        default, 21, 41, 47, 52
        Docker required, 23
        Hello World standalone mode, 27
        init configuring, 27, 52
        querying via Docker, 29
Reliable Actors framework, 96
    invoking, 97
relying partner (RP), 80
reminders and actors, 106
replication of state, 38
    concurrent transactions, 38
    recovery point objective, 38
    replica set, 38
        partition constraint, 39
    scaling stateful services, 39
resources
    ASP .NET integration package, 131
    CloudEvents spec, 60
    code samples in different languages, 24
    components-contrib repository, 24
    consistent hashing whitepaper, 99
    Dapr
        documentation, xi, 20

repository, xi, 23
    security issue submissions, 79
    website, 15
deployment documentation, 31
Kubernetes pods introduction, 21
messaging patterns, 77
Open Enclave SDK, 84
Orleans virtual actors framework, 96
pub/sub example, 63
security documentation, 86
Tollbooth security middleware, 85
Visual Studio code, 129
Zipkin website, 26
retry policies in state management, 42
    Set requests, 43, 53
role-based access control (RBAC), 30
root certificate authority, 91
root spans, 25
routing slip pattern, 74
run
    CLI switches, 25
    Hello World standalone, 25
        testing the application, 29
runtime
    about, 21
    about Dapr, 20
    actor runtime inside Dapr runtime, 99
    edge computing, 146
    function runtime requiring hosting, 147
    Hello World standalone, 25
    host hosting an instance, 21
    max-concurrency switch, 9
    memory use, 19
    repository, xi
    sidecar string IDs, 25
    version, 24
    website for Dapr, 15
Russinovich, Mark, x, 119
Rust, 20

S

SaaS (Software as a Service), 6
Saga pattern, 71
    central coordinator, 71
    events triggering, 72
scaling
    component traits for, 32
    dynamically, 19
    elasticity of cloud, 3, 37, 113

timers and actors, 104
TLS (Transport Layer Security), 89
    (see also mutual TLS)
Token Bucket algorithm, 85
Tollbooth middleware, 85
topics of events, 58
tracing (see distributed tracing)
traits of components, 32
Transactional requests of Dapr state API, 44
transactional state store, 41
Transport Layer Security (TLS), 89
    (see also mutual TLS)
trusted execution environment (TEE), 84
Trusted Root Certificate Authorities store, 91
turn-based concurrency model, 95

U

unified programming model, 19
universal namespace, 12, 143
    application scenarios, 145
    architecture, 144
upgrades in Kubernetes mode, 30
upsert operations in transactions, 44
user identity, 80

V

version, 24
virtual actors, 97
    Dapr actors, 99
virtualization, 4
Visual Studio Dapr code, 129

W

WebAssembly and Dapr, 148

website for Dapr, 15
Woolf, Bobby (Enterprise Integration Patterns
    book), 77
workflows
    actors versus, 124
        (see also actors)
    event-driven, 57
        (see also event-driven programming)
    finite state machine, 124
    message-based, 58
        (see also messaging)

X

X.509 certificates, 90
    requesting, 92
XADD event command, 61
XREAD event command, 61

Y

Yeoman Dapr generator, 128

Z

Zipkin for distributed tracing
    configuration files, 26
    deploying an instance, 27
    exporters for, 26
    Kubernetes
        deploying an instance, 27
        enabling and viewing, 27
    local enabling and viewing, 28
    website, 26
ZooKeeper state store, 47

About the Authors

Haishi Bai works at Microsoft Azure's CTO office and leads various cloud innovation projects. He is an experienced developer and architect with more than 30 years of programming experience. He's also a passionate educator who has published eight cloud computing books and he volunteers at high schools teaching programming languages.

Yaron Schneider is a principal software engineer on Microsoft's Azure CTO team. Yaron has worked for Microsoft for two years as a cloud solution architect, working with large enterprises and startups on high-scale workloads focusing on containers, machine learning, big data and serverless compute, and is now a senior software engineer in CSE. Prior to MS, he served in various engineering roles in startups, and has working knowledge and experience with Google Cloud Platform and AWS. Yaron is an open source contributor and is working on Kubernetes, Terraform and more.

Colophon

The animal on the cover of *Learning Dapr* is a gray marmot (*Marmota baibacina*), a species of rodent in the squirrel family Sciuridae. Gray marmots are one of the largest marmots in the Palearctic, a biogeographic realm that stretches north from the foothills of the Himalayas to the rest of Eurasia. They occupy a range of habitats in this temperate climate zone, from the grasslands of Kyrgyzstan to the top ridges of the Altai and Tian Shan Mountains in Central Asia. While their belly is covered in an orange-reddish brown fur, their dorsal side has a sandy-colored base with brown and black hair tips that give off the grayish appearance that gives them their name.

These very social mammals live in burrows, with multiple burrows forming a colony. Summer burrows are shallow and hold a few individuals, while winter burrows are extensive so that more individuals can hibernate through the winter together.

Each member of a colony plays a role in signaling signs of danger to the rest of the colony, which they do by either making alarm calls or by rapidly moving their tails up and down in the air. Snow leopards, birds of prey, and brown bears are just some of the gray marmot's known predators. For human communities living in the region, gray marmots can be eaten, used in medicine, or sold for their pelts.

Many of the animals on O'Reilly covers are endangered; all of them are important to the world.

The cover illustration is by Karen Montgomery, based on a black and white engraving from the *Museum of Natural History*. The cover fonts are Gilroy Semibold and Guardian Sans. The text font is Adobe Minion Pro; the heading font is Adobe Myriad Condensed; and the code font is Dalton Maag's Ubuntu Mono.

O'REILLY®

There's much more
where this came from.

Experience books, videos, live online
training courses, and more from O'Reilly
and our 200+ partners—all in one place.

Learn more at oreilly.com/online-learning

Lightning Source UK Ltd.
Milton Keynes UK
UKHW031822191222
414174UK00009B/682